THE GOLDEN RETRIEVER

All That Glitters

JULIE CAIRNS

HOWELL BOOK HOUSE

NEW YORK

Howell Book House
A Simon & Schuster Macmillan Company
1633 Broadway
New York, NY 10019-6785

Macmillan Publishing books may be purchased for business or sales promotional use. For information please write: Special Markets Department, Macmillan Publishing USA, 1633 Broadway, New York, NY 10019-6785.

ISBN 0-87605041-0
Library of Congress Cataloging-in-Publication

    Cairns, Julie.
       The golden retriever : all that glitters / Julie Cairns.
         p.   cm.
       Includes bibliographical references (p. 222).
       ISBN 0-87605041-0
       1. Golden retriever. I. Title.
       SF429.G63C35   1998
       636.752'7—dc21   98-22869
                                 CIP

Manufactured in the United States of America
10 9 8 7 6 5 4

Cover and book design by George J. McKeon

Acknowledgments

This book is the result of intense work and valuable contributions from a number of people. The first steps in putting this project together were collecting information on the Golden Retriever Club of America and soliciting requests for photographs from GRCA members throughout the country. This would not have been possible without the help of Jolene Carey, the GRCA administrative assistant.

The information on Goldens and Search and Rescue was provided by Cheryl Gorewitz of Redding, California. She is an active participant with her dog Taylor. A simple request about Search and Rescue resulted in six single-spaced typed pages and enough information to fill a book in itself.

My good friend Carol Kindrick donated her time and grooming shop for help with the chapters on grooming and bathing.

Requests for photographs were sent out to more than 40 GRCA member clubs and at least 500 photographs were received. Most of these are from New York, Missouri, Minnesota and Northern California. Selecting 150 to 200 of these was not an easy task. Decisions on which photos to use were based not only on the quality of the picture, but also on what it depicted. Using the philosophy that a picture tells a thousand words, the primary reason for selection was if a photo fit the text. Many of the contributors included letters that described their deep love and attachment to their Goldens and to the breed in general.

While there are more than 40 contributing photographers in this book, special thanks to Laurie Berman, Andrea Johnson, June Smith and Janis Teichman for their extra efforts in providing outstanding photographs. The photographs in the chapter on the history of the breed are courtesy of Marcia Schlehr and the GRCA Archives. Thanks also to Mary Bloom.

A better understanding and perception of agility is thanks to another friend, Patricia Johnson, who invited me to a club training session. She provided valuable information on the various agility organizations, as well as on therapy dog work.

Thanks to my editor, Beth Adelman of Howell Book House, for giving me the opportunity to write this book. Finally, I must thank my son Alex and husband Tom for giving me the time to complete this project.

Contents

Introduction

Golden Retrievers have been a part of my life for over 25 years. Quite simply, life without one would just not be the same. During the last 20 years we have never had fewer than four of these creatures at any one time.

Most people begin their adventure into the Golden world with a puppy that they bought as a pet. It is usually by pure accident that breed activities are pursued and a lifetime commitment to the breed is developed. This is certainly my story.

My second, third and fourth Goldens led me into obedience, conformation and field training. In 1979 I was a charter member of the Humboldt Dog Obedience Group and became involved in teaching obedience classes through this group. I eventually became a member of the National Association of Dog Obedience Instructors and taught classes for 15 years. My own dogs have earned obedience titles through Utility.

There is nothing quite so exciting as owning a young Golden that lives to retrieve. Finding a way to satisfy this natural desire led to field trials and a growing involvement with hunt tests. I have acted as treasurer and/or secretary of the local retriever field club since 1978. When the AKC Hunt Test program began in 1984, our club held the first sanctioned test on the West Coast.

Since then my primary activity, other than training and running my own dogs, is as a hunt test judge. In 1995 I was honored to be one of three judges at the Master National Retriever Club Test in Addison, Vermont. I am currently on the board of directors of the Master National Club.

As my dogs have always been primarily of field trial stock, my experience in conformation has been limited. Attempts to prove that my good-looking field-bred dogs could be successful in the breed ring were dismal failures.

The Golden Retriever Club of America has been an important part of my life since discovering the truth about dogs. I served as field editor of the *Golden Retriever News* for 10 years and was a co-writer of the breed column in the *AKC Gazette* for two years. Articles I have written also appeared in the now defunct *Hunt Test News*.

As far as practical knowledge about dog care and the importance of responsible breeding, I learned much from volunteer work at the local Humane Society, employment as the secretary for a spay/neuter clinic and three years as a professional dog groomer.

It will be obvious when reading this book that many of the statements regarding the importance of sound structure, temperament and natural retrieving ability are my own opinions. After 25 years of Golden ownership, this, to me, is the most critical aspect of appreciating the breed. I have striven to offer an interpretation that conforms to the ideals of the GRCA and can be understood and appreciated by anyone interested in Golden Retrievers.

Please note that when dogs and their titles are listed, only AKC titles and GRCA recognized titles or awards of achievement are included. Canadian titles have only been included if they are championships. If all the letters seem a bit confusing, have a look at Appendix C for a rundown of what it all means.

JULIE MALOIT-CAIRNS
February 10, 1998

(Laurie Berman)

(Janis Teichman)

CHAPTER 1

Meet the Golden Retriever

It has been more than 20 years since the Golden Retriever emerged from dog breed obscurity to consistently become one of the top five AKC-registered breeds. Despite its immense popularity, the Golden Retriever continues to exhibit the innate personality traits and pleasing looks that make the breed so special to so many dog fanciers, hunters and pet owners. No other breed can fill so many niches, or please so many people with such different needs.

THE FIRST GOLDENS

The Golden Retriever was originally developed in Britain as a hunting dog to retrieve both upland game and waterfowl. The first importers of the breed in North America were avid sportsmen, captivated by the attractive gold-colored retriever that was suitable for so many environments.

The characteristics needed for a suitable hunting retriever describe the desired traits of a Golden Retriever. This is a dog that wants to work with and for its master. The tractable nature of the breed allows it to get along with other hunting dogs and other people. The desire to retrieve anything, especially birds, is inborn. The Golden is a happy, willing worker, whose greatest enjoyment is its work and being with people. The ideal Golden is medium-sized, moderate in coat, with an energy level that fits the occasion, yet calms down easily.

A good hunting retriever will be a great Golden.
(Janis Teichman)

POPULARITY HAS A PRICE

While dedicated Golden fanciers have striven to breed Golden Retrievers that adhere to the traditions of breed type and function, it is more common than ever to find Goldens that do not fit the expected norm. Unfortunately, this is often what happens when a breed becomes too popular. This is not to say that Golden Retrievers that lacked retrieving instincts, disliked people or were overly aggressive and protective did not exist when the breed was relatively unknown. But popularity means that there is a willing market of buyers. Consequently, animals that never would have been bred in the past are now bred to meet the demands of the public.

The fault can not solely be placed on commercial puppy farms or "backyard" breeders. The desire to produce top-winning show dogs and obedience and field trial competitors has also led to the breeding of less than desirable types and temperaments in the name of the betterment of the breed.

What does this mean for someone looking to acquire a Golden Retriever? The answer is to shop carefully. I'll talk more in Chapter 4 about the best place to get a good Golden Retriever.

THE GOLDEN PERSONALITY

No two Golden Retrievers are exactly alike. Anyone who has had a number of Goldens would agree that each is a unique individual. The common thread that unites individuals within the breed is the love of people and life in general. The Golden will greet a complete stranger as a long lost friend. It is a rare Golden that takes any warming up, and it is not their nature to be scared of or aggressive towards people.

Extreme friendliness is a trait that is endearing to many, yet can be a detriment if you're looking for a dog that is oriented to an individual or a single family. It's something to consider before you get a Golden.

A Golden is more than satisfactory as an alarm system and is quite willing to bark at disturbances or the arrival of strangers. This is as far as it goes, however, for while the Golden will bark, its tail will be wagging in greeting. It will then most likely lead the stranger inside. Golden owners often joke that the dog will then proceed to show the stranger where the silver is kept.

Goldens also love to be the center of attention and may be quite demanding about it. A hand holding a drink is fair game to be flipped with a wet nose. Chairs and couches are natural places to sit and lie on for dogs that consider themselves to be people. Their tails always seem to be wagging. These are the little things that make Goldens special. When these personality traits are channeled properly and viewed with a sense of humor, they can

Each one of these dogs will have a unique personality. (Janis Teichman)

create endless enjoyment for both dog and owner. However, if you want a dog with a more serious nature, or if you tend to be pretty serious yourself, you may not find these traits to your liking.

NATURAL INSTINCTS

This zest for living makes for a dog that finds great joy in making life fun. If there is something to jump over, a hole to explore, something new to retrieve, a Golden will find it. They love to show off and parade around with something that usually is not theirs.

A common trait among many Goldens is to grab an arm and lead its owner on a tour. The desire to retrieve may be overpowering and almost

This gang of four might bark, but no one would be afraid of them. Goldens do not make good guard dogs. (June Smith)

anything may be fetched by a Golden. Pots and pans, clothing, toys, dirty underwear, books—the list is endless. This instinct can be curbed with maturity and training, but when you first get your dog, it may be necessary to keep things out of reach.

The retrieving trait often goes along with a mouthiness problem. Many Goldens, especially when they are young, could be categorized as destructive in their chewing habits. They can and will destroy anything that they can get their mouths around. Dogs with this inclination must be given their own chewing materials and have everything else kept out of their reach.

Another necessary trait for a successful sporting dog is the instinct to chase prey. This is called prey drive, and it makes a good field dog. However, this same drive, when applied to a pet situation, means that small animals, such as cats, bunnies and even small dogs, when they take flight are game to a retriever.

Golden Retriever breeders regularly receive puppy inquiries from people who have been informed that Goldens are good pets for those who live around livestock and poultry. This is an accident waiting to happen. The only way such an arrangement can work is if the dog is in a fenced area and the poultry or livestock are in a separate enclosure.

Related to chasing is digging, and Goldens make champion diggers. Most digging is done in the pursuit of gophers and moles. Then, when they learn how much fun it is to dig, they just do it for pure enjoyment.

There are many naturally very well-behaved Goldens in the world who retrieve, chew, dig and chase in moderation and are trained to curtail

Goldens have been bred to retrieve, and they need an outlet for their natural urge. (Beth Adelman)

these vices with a minimum of effort. It is because of this that so many people want to add a Golden to their family. But many people fail to realize that

Advanced obedience work includes jumping and retrieving. This is Am./Can. Ch. Cobrador's Hijo de Espana, CD, CGC, going over the high jump. (Tom Bailey)

Goldens are dogs with some very dog-like habits that were bred into them for a reason. These dogs need training and outlets for their inborn characteristics. Unfortunately, it is more likely that dogs with these problems will end up in animal shelters and become one among the millions of unwanted dogs in the country.

THE PERFECT MEDIUM-SIZE DOG

The Golden can be the ideal dog for someone looking for an active, athletic, medium-size companion. The breed standard describes the male Golden as weighing 65 to 75 pounds and the female as weighing 55 to 65 pounds.

In reality, there are plenty of dogs of both sexes that are much larger or much smaller than called for in the standard. Golden Retrievers that are 28 inches tall and over 100 pounds are not uncommon, as are 20-inch females that weigh 45 pounds. (A dog's height is measured from the ground to the withers, which is the point on the back just above the shoulder.) There are breeders who favor either end of the size spectrum, and both large and small dogs have been outstanding competitors and producers.

The Golden of proper size is best suited for the tasks it was originally bred

A Golden of proper size is best suited for the tasks it was bred to perform. (Laurie Berman)

to perform. It is large enough to withstand the rigors encountered in a day's hunt, yet not so large that it tires easily and is clumsy in its efforts.

Extremely large Goldens may have more physical difficulties if they are not soundly put together and are more likely to break down and age prematurely. An extremely active large dog is much more difficult to live with and train than a smaller dog. This is a serious consideration when looking at one's resources, abilities and living situation.

CLOTHING: COLOR AND COAT

The defining characteristic of the Golden Retriever is its coat. The color itself ranges from shades of nearly white to almost red. While there is no absolutely correct color, the Golden of medium gold that glistens in the sun and blends in with the colors of fall is best suited for the purposes of a hunting dog. This color, when combined with a slightly wavy coat, is perfect camouflage in many hunting situations.

When it comes to how a Golden behaves, performs or trains, the color has no bearing. It should be the last consideration in selection or evaluation. While everyone has their own personal preference, whether a Golden is a blonde or a redhead should make little difference.

The texture, density and length of the coat is far more important and has far more bearing on everyday life with a Golden. There is great diversity in Golden coat types. What actually exists varies greatly from what is described in the standard. The ideal Golden coat is medium in length and lies close to the body. It is comprised of a dense, soft undercoat with longer, darker guard hairs that act as an outer coat. The feathering on the back of the legs and tail is longer than the coat covering the body. The harsher outer coat acts as a sort of barrier to moisture. A Golden with a proper coat can emerge from the water, shake and appear nearly dry.

Ch. Smithaven's Firm Fav O'Rhet, CD, WCX (left), and Smithaven's Loquacious Luke, WC. These are Goldens of moderate color and coat with extremely attractive heads. (June Smith)

The ideal coat is relatively trouble free and stays nice looking with a minimum of regular brushing. But Golden coats are often much heavier and longer than is called for in the standard. These coats often require extensive brushing to keep them attractive and free of mats.

Regardless of the length or thickness of coat, all Golden Retrievers usually shed twice a year, depending on their health and the weather conditions. One of these shedding periods is usually much heavier than the other, leaving the dog looking like a mere image of itself until the new coat grows in. During the shedding period, the soft undercoat seems to fall out in chunks, leaving hair everywhere. During the remainder of the year, hair is lost in small increments and is found on the floor, covering the couch or wherever a Golden may seek a resting place.

GOLDENS AND CHILDREN

The Golden Retriever is sometimes considered the "perfect" family dog. It is true that most Goldens are good with children and would rather hang out with a child than anyone else in the world.

However, not all Goldens are good with children and not all children are good with dogs of any kind. It is not uncommon for the average dog to view a young child as another dog, and treat them as such. The child is on the floor, it takes anything it can find and puts things in its mouth, and it makes demands on a dog that the animal often does not understand. It is no wonder that children often become the victim of dog bites. That's why anyone with very young children

Golden Retrievers enjoying a day at the beach near San Francisco. (Laurie Berman)

should only obtain a Golden, puppy or adult, if they are very experienced with dogs.

As children become older, they can unknowingly be cruel to dogs, and some very unfair and dangerous situations may arise. It is also not fair to obtain a puppy for a child and expect them to take responsibility for it. Children rarely understand this type of obligation. A dog should be for the entire family, with adults taking on the primary duties of feeding, training and grooming while children enjoy the companionship of a good friend and learn about responsible dog ownership.

Another major concern is that growing families just don't have the time to give a Golden the attention it requires. Make sure you're ready for a dog before you take one on.

WHAT EVERY GOLDEN NEEDS

If Golden Retrievers were asked what they needed for a satisfactory lifestyle, their number one response would be attention. They want to be a part of their human's life.

Exercise and being included in the activities of others make Goldens happy. (Lorraine Rodolph)

Goldens enjoy being outdoors in a fenced yard, but they like it better when you're there with them, and look forward to the time spent indoors with you. They enjoy helping with food preparation, and participation in your meal is important to their life. They like to watch television and play games with the family. A pet on the head or under the chin, a rubbed stomach, a shake of the paw are all important to a Golden.

Attention should also take the form of training. Basic obedience—sit, down, come and stay—is essential in the life of any happy, well-balanced retriever. Training can also include learning a job or refining a skill. This most commonly involves retrieving, but there are many other outlets for the talents of a Golden—the list is long. One may choose to pursue organized dog events of some type, such as obedience, hunting tests, tracking, agility or even flyball. Goldens are frequent visitors at rest homes and care centers as registered therapy dogs, and work as assistance dogs for the handicapped. The possibilities are numerous.

Daily exercise is another form of attention a Golden would say is vital. This can be a walk, a run, multiple long retrieves or swimming, and can be combined with training.

Next on their list would be security. Included here is at least one outstanding meal a day of top-quality dog food. A good dog biscuit added a couple of times a day to keep a dog going is high on the list. A secure and comfortable place to sleep is a must. A completely fenced yard or dog area to hang out in when not supervised or when the folks are gone is necessary. This area should have a covering of some type for protection from weather.

A dog crate is another essential a Golden would include. These make ideal places to sit in when in the car and are good places to get away from everyone once in awhile. A Golden also feels secure when it has a few things of its own. These could include a toy, a good knucklebone, a hard rubber ball—such things go a long way towards making a dog happy.

Finally, the Golden would say that it needs care. This includes visits to the veterinarian for shots and check-ups. Flea, tick and heartworm preventives are necessary in many parts of the country. Grooming is another necessity for a dog. The brushing is fun and almost falls under the category of attention, as does ear cleaning. A Golden would readily admit that these should be done quite regularly. However, nail clipping is not always fun, but does feel better afterwards and makes running and jumping easier.

Few breeds of dog can offer so much in the way of enjoyment, all-around usefulness, ease of training and care. Once one has had a Golden Retriever, life is never quite the same without one. There is a tremendous diversity within the breed as far as color, coat and size, yet despite these differences these dogs are all Golden Retrievers because they share the personality traits that unite individuals and make them identifiable as a single breed. Understanding them and what makes them work is a constant source of wonder.

(Chuck Lee)

CHAPTER 2

A History of the Golden Retriever

Retrievers became popular in Britain in the 1800s with the growth of the sport of hunting. They were considered the elite of the sporting breeds because they were so versatile and could be successfully used for both upland game and waterfowl. Many breeds were crossed during this time, and there is no doubt that many types of retrievers existed before the actual development of the Golden Retriever. Some of these dogs were very much like Goldens in appearance.

Sir Dudley Majoribanks, later known as Lord Tweedmouth, is given credit for the actual creation of the Golden Retriever, thanks to his breeding program in Scotland in the mid- to late 1800s. All modern-day Goldens can trace their origins to Lord Tweedmouth's foundation stock.

Lord Tweedmouth acquired a young male yellow Wavy (Flat) Coated Retriever in 1866, known as Nous. The yellow color is due to a recessive gene, and an occasional yellow puppy still occurs in litters of the Flat Coated Retriever. Photos of Nous show that he was a wavy coated dog and looked very much like a modern Golden Retriever.

The other half of Lord Tweedmouth's first breeding was a Tweed Water Spaniel bitch named Belle. This variety of Water Spaniel was a favorite hunting dog of the area. These dogs were known for their swimming ability, superior intelligence and wonderful temperaments. They were medium in size, liver

Black Game, artist unknown. This is an old print from Liverpool that dates back to 1857. The dog in the front has many characteristics of a Golden Retriever.

colored (any shade of yellow to brown) and had a tightly curled coat with very little feathering. All retriever breeds share a similar genetic origin. One of the things that separates the Golden from the other retriever breeds is this Tweed Water Spaniel ancestry. The traits ascribed to this breed closely resemble many of the ones we hold so dear in the Golden Retriever.

The breeding of Nous and Belle in 1868 resulted in four yellow puppies: Ada, Crocus, Cowslip and Primrose. Lord Tweedmouth kept Cowslip for his planned breeding program. She was then bred to Tweed, another Tweed Water Spaniel, and later to Sampson, a Red Setter. The second breeding is thought to have been done to improve scenting abilities and to fix color.

In 1884 a second yellow dog named Nous was whelped. This dog's sire was Jack, a son of Sampson and Cowslip. His dam was Zoe, whose sire was a black Flat Coat and whose dam was Topsy, a daughter of Tweed and Cowslip. The final pedigree

entered in Lord Tweedmouth's stud book is the breeding of the second Nous to Queenie. Queenie was the daughter of a black Flat Coat and Gill, a littermate to the second Nous. Two yellow puppies, Prim and Rose, resulted from this breeding. These two are the link between Lord Tweedmouth's original dogs and today's Golden.

During this time there were other sportsmen who obtained dogs from Lord Tweedmouth and no doubt bred Golden type dogs, but none kept the detailed records necessary to document a formal breeding program.

The first Goldens were registered in Britain in 1904 and were listed along with the Wavy or Flat Coated Retrievers. After 1913 they were separated by color and known as Golden or Yellow Retrievers. The term Golden Retriever was not recognized until 1920.

Goldens first made their appearance in field trials in the early 1900s and achieved some success. At the same time, some early fanciers began entering their dogs in conformation shows. Lord Harcourt was an important early breeder who used the Culham prefix on his dogs. His foundation pair, Culham Brass and Culham Rossa, were descendants of Prim and Rose.

A grandson of Brass and Rossa, Ch. Noranby Campfire, born in 1913, was the first dog to complete a breed championship. Mrs. Charlesworth owned this dog and was a driving force in the breed until the 1950s. Her dogs were registered with the Noranby Kennel name.

The World Wars seriously undermined the growth and quality of the breed. In these periods breeding came to a standstill, and all dog activities

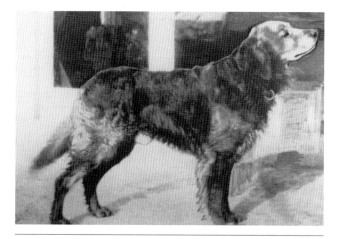

Eng. Ch. Noranby Campfire (Culham Copper out of Normanby Beauty) at nine years of age. This photo was taken in 1921 at the field trial where he won his working qualifier, making him the first champion Golden.

ceased. During World War II some breeders sent their stock to the United States for safety. Following the wars there was a serious drop in quality, as anything that looked like a Golden Retriever was bred to satisfy the demand.

An interest in lighter-colored dogs began in the 1930s (before then most Goldens were dark gold). Eventually, the breed standard was changed to allow for light- or cream-colored dogs. This would eventually have an impact on how Goldens looked worldwide.

GOLDENS IN AMERICA

Golden Retrievers first appeared in the United States as early as the 1890s. There are photographs of Lord Tweedmouth's son, the Hon. Archie Majoribanks, at his ranch in Texas with Lady, who was a descendant of Lord Tweedmouth's dogs. She was reportedly the grandam of Lord Harcourt's Culham Brass. There are other reports of Goldens in Canada and the United States in the early 1900s, but none of them were ever registered.

The breed did not make its official entry into the United States until the 1920s. This was a period when Americans were enamored of anything British, including their sporting traditions and dogs. Along with Labrador Retrievers, a few Goldens were imported by some of America's most prominent citizens.

Robert Appleton, a resident of East Hampshire, Long Island, was the retired head of a publishing company. In 1925 he was the first to actually register a Golden Retriever with the American Kennel Club. This was an imported three-year-old male named Lomberdale Blondin. He also imported and registered a female, Dan Hill Judy. These two produced the first registered litter in December 1925.

However, Goldens did not gain recognition as a separate breed until 1932. Before that year, they were shown with Labrador Retrievers in the dog shows. During this interval, some dogs were shown sporadically and there was an occasional litter of puppies. But none of these dogs had any influence on the breed as it developed in this country.

Dr. Charles Large of New York City was the first serious Golden breeder in the United States. In 1931 he imported a number of dogs from Britain that were shown and became the foundation of his breeding program. His kennel name was Fernova, and he was an early activist in the attempt to form a national breed club. His efforts were not

Eng. Ch. Noranby Deirdre, born in 1933, was sired by Ch. Heydown Grip out of Ch. Noranby Diana. She was later exported to this country.

realized when he died in 1933. Most of his dogs were passed on to Michael Clemens, who continued Large's breeding under the kennel name Frantelle.

Goldens of this era were owned exclusively by the wealthy. They were primarily obtained out of curiosity and for the breed's growing reputation as an outstanding hunting dog. Few actually lived in the average home or were acquired as pets. They were generally found in large kennel facilities overseen by kennel managers.

It is an interesting side note that a Golden was entered in the first AKC Licensed Retriever Field Trial held on Long Island in 1931. This young female, who had been imported from Britain, was one of two entered in the Puppy Stake, and went on to beome Ch. Lady Burns.

The Golden breed received the boost it needed when Col. Samuel Magoffin of Vancouver, British Columbia, imported Speedwell Pluto from Britain in 1932. He become a champion in both the United States and Canada and was the first Golden Retriever to win a Best in Show ribbon. Pluto was not just a show dog and was hunted hard off the rugged coast of the Pacific Northwest. He is considered to be the foundation sire of the breed in America, though he only sired one litter that was whelped in the United States.

Magoffin's Rockhaven Kennels were based in Vancouver, but he had another kennel located in Englewood, Colorado, called Gilnockie. And Pluto was not his only import that would be influential in the development of the breed. Magoffin had relatives in Minnesota and Wisconsin that followed his lead in obtaining Goldens.

Ralph Boalt of Winona, Minnesota, was Magoffin's brother-in-law. He imported a bitch from Britain, Patience of Yelme, who was the beginning of Stilrovin Kennels. Stilrovin is most famous for Gilnockie Coquette, who was bred at Magoffin's Colorado kennel. By two different sires she produced three field champions, a dual champion and a bench champion. These dogs, FC Stilrovin Super Speed, FC Stilrovin Nito Express, FC Stilrovin Katherine, Dual Ch. Stilrovin Rip's Pride and Ch. Stilrovin Shur Shot, were among the most influential producers as the breed gained recognition and popularity in the late 1940s.

At about the same time, Ben Boalt, Ralph's brother, started Beavertail Kennels across the border in Wisconsin. The kennel name was later changed to Gunnerman. His stock was of Rockhaven lineage.

Another early Golden fancier in the Minnesota area was Henry Christian. Goldwood Kennels had its start in 1933 with a bitch imported from Britain named Sprite of Aldgrove and a Pluto son from Canada named Rockhaven Rory. Both completed their championships and ran field trials. Rory was an early member of the Show Dog Hall of Fame and was one of the most widely used stud dogs among breeders in the region. Goldwood Kennels produced FC Goldwood Tuck and two of the first great Golden obedience competitors: Goldwood Michael, UD, and Goldwood Toby, UD. Toby was the first Golden to earn a Utility title.

The St. Louis, Missouri, area was another region of early Golden activity. Mr. and Mrs. Mahlon Wallace, Jr., and John K. Wallace began importing from Britain in 1933. The breeding of two of their imports, Speedwell Reuben and Ch. Speedwell Tango, resulted in the great FC Rip. In 1939 he was the first Golden to complete a field championship. Even today, his record of consistency and points earned in Open stakes holds up as one of the best in the breed. Equally impressive is the fact that he was owner-amateur handled in an era when almost all dogs were handled by professionals.

John Wallace used the kennel name White-bridge on his dogs. When World War II broke out in Europe, many dogs from Britain's Yelme Kennels went to Wallace. Some of these dogs did well in American field trials and became successful producers of working dogs. One important import

FC Rip was the breed's first field champion in 1939. He amassed over 60 Open points in a two-year period, before his death at the age of six.

was Eng./Am. Ch. Bingo of Yelme. Bingo was a successful field trial competitor as well as a champion. He is best remembered as the sire of Boalt's great producer, Gilnockie Coquette.

Eng. Ch. Marine of Woolley was another British import who influenced the development of the working Golden. He was imported and owned by Blue Leader Kennels in Santa Barbara, California, and was one of the first Goldens in that part of the country. Marine sired the littermates Rockhaven Ben Bolt and Rockhaven Judy, both of whom ended up in Minnesota. Ben Bolt was owned by Ralph Boalt and run in field trials. He was a popular sire during the late 1930s and early 1940s. Judy was one of the foundation bitches of Woodend Kennels in Minnesota. She produced several top field dogs that would become

Eng./Am. Ch. Bingo of Yelme*** was born in 1933 and brought to this country three years later. He was a Best of Breed winner as well as a qualified all-age field dog.

important as the breed gained popularity as a field competitor. Woodend Kennels is also notable for having bred NFC King Midas of Woodend. He was the first National Field Champion in 1941.

The growth and popularity of the Golden in the Midwest during these years was truly a phenomenon. The breed was embraced by an increasing number of hunters as the dog for the job. Through the mid-1940s half of the Golden litters registered by the American Kennel Club were whelped in southeastern Minnesota.

It was through the efforts of the Midwestern fanciers that the Golden Retriever Club of America was formed in 1939. John Wallace was the first club president. The club has long been the

guiding force in ensuring that the breed standard, character and original purpose are upheld.

After World War II the breed saw increased growth, and Goldens could be found in almost every part of the country. More Americans now had the money and leisure time to include a dog in the family. However, Goldens were still relatively unknown to the general public as a pet. The majority were still in the hands of show and field competitors or hunters.

There is not enough space to list the many great Goldens and breeders that have contributed to the growth and development of the breed over the years. But we should mention a few. The great AFC Ch. Lorelei's Golden Rockbottom, UD, (Ch. Lorelei's Golden Rip** out of Lorelei's Golden

One of the great Goldens of the 1950s was the talented and good looking AFC Ch. Lorelei's Golden Rockbottom, UD.

Tanya) stands alone in his record of achievements. (Asterisks after a dog's name denote field trial placements. See Appendix C for more on what they mean.) He was owned and bred by Reinhard Bischoff. In addition to his Amateur Field Championship, Rocky, as he was known, was a member of the Show Dog Hall of Fame, a High in Trial Winner and an Outstanding Sire, though he became sterile at the age of three.

Rocky's son, Ch. Little Joe of Tigathoe***, was owned and bred by Mrs. George Flinn, Jr. He continued producing where his sire left off. Joe had group placements and field trial placements. He was one of the important sires of the 1950s and is behind most show and field lines.

Mrs. George Flinn, Jr., known as Torch, has owned more Golden field champions than anyone, with ten to her credit. Her last FC completed its title a year after her death in 1996. Flinn bred many great Goldens over a period of involvement that lasted six decades. In the early 1970s she and Mrs. Robert Sadler were responsible for breeding FC/AFC Bonnie Brooks Elmer to Tigathoes Chickasaw. The resulting litter included three field champions and the breed's last dual champion, AFC and Dual Ch. Tigathoe's Funky Farquar.

FOR BETTER OR WORSE

Different trends and fads have taken their toll on the breed over the years, and genetic problems began to surface that would have an impact on the course of many breeding programs. During the 1950s Goldens became increasingly larger, especially in height. Golden Retrievers were becoming popular

FC/AFC Stilrovin Tuppee Tee (Stilrovin Bearcat out of Pink Lady of Audlon**) was from the Stilrovin breeding that produced three FC/AFCs in the 1960s. She was one of the breed's great Golden female field champions.

that reached 28 inches at the withers and resembled Setters more than Retrievers. This was the reason height limits were added to the breed standard.

Golden Retrievers with lameness in the hindquarters also became increasingly common. Through research this problem was discovered to be hip dysplasia. Initially, a council was formed within the Golden Retriever Club of America to research this problem, and concerned Golden breeders began to X-ray their stock in the mid-1960s. The Orthopedic Foundation for Animals (OFA), which keeps hip dysplasia records for all breeds, was set up largely through the impetus of the GRCA.

Since the late 1960s, routine hip X-rays and evaluations from OFA have greatly reduced the

Ch. Little Joe of Tigathoe*** and his owner/breeder Torch Flinn. Joe was a son of Rocky and is behind most field and show lines.

frequency and severity of hip dysplasia in the breed. Over a nearly 30-year period more than 60,000 Golden Retrievers have received OFA ratings for fair, good or excellent hips.

At about the same time as hip investigation became important, it also became obvious that Goldens had genetic eye problems, primarily cataracts. Routine eye exams became a part of screening for any breeding stock.

IMPORTANT IMPORTS

American breeders have continued to import Goldens from Britain, and while few imported dogs have had any impact on the breed, during the late 1960s and early 1970s several imports began to make a difference. The greatest change was that lighter-color coats were seen more frequently. The light color became increasingly popular with show fanciers, and then with the general public.

The imported dogs were also different in overall type than the darker American Golden that had been developed from earlier British stock of a different era.

During this same period, two half brothers, Ch. Misty Morn's Sunset CD, TD, WC, (known as Sammy), and Am./Can./Bda. Ch. Cummings' Gold-Rush Charlie, began a trend towards developing a more consistent type in show Goldens. Sammy still holds the record for number of champions and titled dogs produced. Charlie was the all-time high point Golden show dog with 38 Best in Show wins, and is still the only Golden Retriever to be named top show dog in the

Sporting group, a distinction he earned in 1974. Charlie was equally important as a sire. His show record was broken in 1993 by Am./Can. Ch. Asterling's Wild Blue Yonder.

One British import of the 1970s made such a great impact that he almost completely changed the direction of field-bred Goldens. Barbara Howard purchased Holway Barty at about a year of age and had him running in licensed field trials within a few months. He won a Derby Stake, and people took immediate note of this flashy little dog. Barty went on to complete his Amateur Field Championship, completely owner trained and handled.

His impact on the breed was in his prepotency as a sire. Barty produced nine field champions, several obedience trial champions and more working titled offspring than any other Golden.

Am./Can./Bda. Ch. Cummings' Gold-Rush Charlie (Ch. Sunset's Happy Duke out of Ch. Cummings' Golden Princess) was the top winning Sporting show dog in 1974. He was also an outstanding producer.

One of his sons was NAFC/FC Topbrass Cotton (out of Ch. Sunstream Gypsy of Topbrass). In addition to being on the National Derby List, he was a Double Header Winner and is the all-time high point field trial Golden with 274 points and was the first Golden to win the National Amateur Retriever Championship.

Before Barty, no Golden had sired more than five field champions. He sired over 63 outstanding offspring, including eight field champions. He also added a consistency in marking, style and trainability that was missing or laying dormant in many Golden lines.

NAFC/FC Topbrass Cotton with his breeder, co-owner and handler Jackie Mertens. Cotton was the first Golden to win the National Amateur Retriever Trial.

denominator in terms of the genetic background of a successful obedience dog. The real necessary ingredients are soundness and a willing attitude.

As mentioned earlier, until the 1970s the Golden was not a well-known breed. They were a well-kept secret, often confused with the very popular Irish Setter. The event that brought the Golden Retriever prominence with the American public took place in 1974, when President Gerald Ford obtained a Golden female. Liberty and her subsequent litter of White House puppies received national publicity.

The secret was out. Goldens skyrocketed in popularity and were ranked among the top five in registrations. This situation has remained constant for 20 years. While it is a sign that the Golden is not just a fad, popularity is of constant concern to everyone involved with the breed.

It is important to keep in mind the breed's early history, original intent and purpose as a hunting dog and companion. A common theme of concern has been that the breed has split into

A SECRET NO LONGER

It was also during the 1970s that Goldens emerged as one of the premier breeds for obedience competition. When the Obedience Trial Champion title was established in July 1977, the first three dogs of any breed to earn the title were Golden Retrievers. Since then, Goldens have earned that title more often than any other breed. There is no common two, three or even more distinct types with different purposes. Unfortunately, this has already occurred to some extent. The Golden has been adapted and bred to succeed in the various phases of dog competition. Not very long ago, Goldens that were successful in different activities came from the same litter. Dogs whose primary purpose was hunting could compete in the show ring, and many show champions were good field dogs. While even at that time there were extremes at either end of the type spectrum, the breed as a whole was considered dual purpose.

Today, that is not always the case. Many are of the belief that field-bred dogs no longer resemble Golden Retrievers. There are just as many who believe that the strictly bench-bred dog's excessive coat and bone make it unfit as a working dog.

Serious breeders strive to produce a Golden that fits the standard in all ways and can be used for a variety of purposes. This is the lesson our breed's history should teach us.

(Janis Teichman)

CHAPTER 3

Understanding the Breed Standard

A breed standard is a written description of how an ideal specimen of a breed should look. All dogs are evaluated according to how they measure up to the description in the standard. It is a list of all the little details that differentiate one breed from another and determine type.

Type is a nearly indescribable quality that makes a dog a true specimen of its breed. A dog may possess every desired characteristic described in the standard, but if it is lacking in type it is just another dog. Conversely, a dog may be faulty in many aspects but have excellent type. Type is expressed in character, expression and many minute details that add up to a Golden Retriever.

When reading the standard and attempting to evaluate your dog, remember that the perfect dog has yet to be born. A dog can fit the breed standard in every aspect and possess good type, yet not be of show quality. The breed standard for Golden Retrievers follows, with comments in italics.

OFFICIAL STANDARD FOR THE GOLDEN RETRIEVER

GENERAL APPEARANCE: A symmetrical, powerful, active dog, sound and well put together, not clumsy nor long in the leg, displaying a kindly expression and possessing a personality that is eager, alert and self-confident. Primarily a

Dogs are typically evaluated in this stacked show stance. (June Smith)

hunting dog, he should be shown in hard working condition. Overall appearance, balance, gait and purpose to be given more emphasis than any of his component parts.

The Golden Retriever is first and foremost a sporting dog. It was developed for the purpose of hunting and should always exhibit the structure and traits required of a working dog. A golden-colored dog with lots of coat is not necessarily a Golden Retriever.

FAULTS: Any departure from the described ideal shall be considered faulty to the degree to which it interferes with the breed's purpose or is contrary to breed character.

A fault is a deviation from the correct condition. Some faults will not interfere with a dog's function as a working dog, but are not typical of the breed. An obvious example

would be a Golden with large splotches of black hair in its coat. While the color of hair will not affect the dog's ability to work, it is very faulty in that the dog does not look like a Golden Retriever.

SIZE, PROPORTION, SUBSTANCE: Males 23 to 24 inches in height at withers; females 21 ½ to 22 ½ inches. Dogs up to one inch above or below standard size should be proportionately penalized. Deviation in height of more than one inch from the standard shall disqualify. Length from breastbone to point of buttocks slightly greater than height at withers in a ratio of 12:11. Weight for dogs, 65 to 75 pounds; bitches, 55 to 65 pounds.

The height is measured at the withers. The withers is the highest part of the back where the shoulder meets the neck. The dog should stand on a level surface with a flat object placed on the withers. A measuring stick is held up

A dive of this quality requires a sound body and hard working condition. (Janis Teichman)

A balanced and well put together puppy gives a hint of future promise. (Cheryl Baca)

above, slightly deeper and wider at stop than at tip. No heaviness in flews. Removal of whiskers is permitted but not preferred.

The head of the Golden should be strong enough in structure to carry birds. A head can be less than perfect and still be quite functional and even very attractive if it is balanced proportionately.

and the height is determined by where the bottom of the flat object touches the ruler.

The reason for the height restriction is to keep the Golden a medium-size dog. Goldens that are good specimens in every aspect except height exist at both ends of the size spectrum. But if the breed is allowed to become too tall or too short, it may be ineffective in function according to its original purpose.

Weight must be proportional to bone structure and height. A small bitch that is at the low end of the standard would be fat at 65 pounds. An extremely muscular dog will often weigh more than a larger dog that carries fat. The overall appearance and look of the dog is more important than the actual weight.

HEAD: Broad in skull, slightly arched laterally and longitudinally without prominence of frontal bones (forehead) or occipital bones. *Stop* well defined but not abrupt. *Foreface* deep and wide, nearly as long as skull. *Muzzle* straight in profile, blending smooth and strongly into skull; when viewed in profile or from

A classic Golden head. Note the pigment, stop and proportion of muzzle to head. (June Smith)

A Golden of darker color and of field breeding with excellent balance, pigment and expression. (Janis Teichman)

EYES: Friendly and intelligent in expression, medium large with dark, close-fitting rims, set well apart and reasonably deep in sockets. Color preferably dark brown; medium brown acceptable. Slant eyes and narrow, triangular eyes detract from correct expression and are to be faulted. No white or haw visible when looking straight ahead. Dogs showing evidence of functional abnormality of eyelids or eyelashes (such as, but not limited to, trichiasis, entropion, ectropion, or distichiasis) are to be excused from the ring.

It is the eyes that make the Golden Retriever special. The eyes express the intelligence, personality and soul of the dog. The nicest head can be ruined by light eyes, which give a harsh expression to the face. A weak head can be saved by dark, expressive eyes.

EARS: Rather short with front edge attached well behind and just above the eye and falling close to cheek. When pulled forward, tip of ear should just cover the eye. Low, hound-like ear set to be faulted.

The ear placement is as much a part of the expression of the Golden as its eyes and facial features. Extremely large ears are unattractive, and dogs with small ears that are placed too high on the head are atypical of the breed.

NOSE: Black or brownish black, though fading to a lighter shade in cold weather not serious. Pink nose or one seriously lacking in pigmentation to be faulted. *Teeth* scissors bite, in which the outer side of the lower incisors touches the inner side of the upper incisors. Undershot or overshot bite is a *disqualification.* Misalignment of teeth (irregular placement of incisors) or a level bite (incisors meet each other edge to edge) is undesirable, but not to be confused with undershot or overshot. Full dentition. Obvious gaps are *serious faults.*

In an undershot bite, the teeth of the lower jaw protrude beyond the upper jaw. An overshot bite is the reverse of this condition. Missing teeth is a genetic trait, and in some instances is associated with other abnormalities. The

Another head of a different type, but equally correct in proportion and expression. (Janis Teichman)

presence of extra premolars is linked to the same gene that produces missing teeth. Large gaps with missing teeth are unattractive and indicative of other problems. Missing teeth also mean the dog will have trouble holding objects in the mouth—a primary function of retrievers.

NECK, TOPLINE, BODY: *Neck* medium long, merging gradually into well laid back shoulders, giving sturdy, muscular appearance. No throatiness. *Backline* strong and level from withers to slightly sloping croup, whether standing or moving. Sloping backline, roach or sway back, flat or steep croup to be faulted. *Body* well balanced, short coupled, deep through the chest. Chest between forelegs at least as wide as a man's closed hand including thumb, with well developed forechest. Brisket extends to elbow. Ribs long and well sprung but not barrel shaped, extending well towards hindquarters. Loin short, muscular, wide and deep, with very little tuck-up. Slab-sidedness, narrow chest, lack of depth in brisket, excessive tuck-up to be *faulted.*

A well-placed neck and solid body structure are basic requirements for any working retriever. Weak neck placement makes it difficult for a dog to carry a bird. A long bodied, weakly put together dog will not be able to withstand the rigors of a day in the field.

TAIL: Well set on, thick and muscular at the base, following the natural line of the croup. Tail bones extend to, but not below, the point of hock. Carried with merry action, level or with some moderate upward curve; never curled over back nor between legs.

Tails can be placed correctly or incorrectly for the most attractive appearance. How the dog carries its tail in certain situations is an indication of its temperament. A dog that carries the tail over its back when other dogs are around may be aggressively inclined. The tail that is tucked between the legs indicates a dog that is fearful of its surroundings and may be spooky and lacking in confidence.

A correct front assembly is essential for a working dog. The length of neck, proper placement in relation to the shoulder and correct angulation make carrying a duck easy. (Barbara Taylor)

FOREQUARTERS: Muscular, well coordinated with hindquarters and capable of free movement. *Shoulder blades* long and well laid back with upper tips fairly close together at withers. *Upper arms* appear about the same length as the blades, setting the elbows back beneath the upper tip of the blades, close to the ribs without looseness. *Legs*, viewed from the front, straight with good bone, but not to the point of coarseness. *Pasterns* short and strong, sloping slightly with no suggestion of weakness. Dewclaws on forelegs may be removed, but are normally left on.

The front assembly is essential to a sound working retriever, and at the same time is the most difficult to understand and maintain. The front of the dog takes the most abuse when working, which is why a properly put together front end is so important for the endurance and working life of the dog.

Dewclaws are removed to prevent tearing during field work. It is a simple procedure if done when puppies are a few days old, and can prevent future injuries.

FEET: medium size, round compact, and well knuckled, with thick pads. Excess hair may be trimmed to show natural size and contour. Splayed or hare feet to be faulted.

Tightly put together feet can withstand hours of work and are less susceptible to cuts and other forms of injury in the field. Many apparently splayed feet can be helped or prevented by keeping the nails short.

HINDQUARTERS: Broad and strongly muscled. Profile of croup slopes slightly; the pelvic bone slopes at a slightly greater angle (approximately 30 degrees from horizontal). In a natural stance, the femur joins the pelvis at approximately a 90-degree angle; *stifles* well bent; *hocks* well let down with short, strong *rear pasterns*. *Feet* as in front. *Legs* straight when viewed from rear. Cow-hocks, spread hocks, and sickle hocks to be *faulted*.

Angulation of the rear quarters is as difficult to appreciate and understand as that of the forequarters. While the ideal angulation is best suited for work, dogs do quite well with less than perfect angulation as long as they are balanced. The angulation of front and rear is equal, giving the dog a look of overall harmony.

COAT: Dense and water-repellent with good undercoat. Outer coat firm and resilient, neither coarse nor silky, lying close to body; may be straight or wavy. Untrimmed natural ruff; moderate feathering on back of forelegs and on underbody; heavier feathering on front of neck, back of thighs and underside of tail. Coat on head, paws, and front of legs is short and even. Excessive length, open coats, and limp, soft coats are very undesirable. Feet may be trimmed and stray hairs neatened, but the natural appearance of coat or outline should not be altered by cutting or clipping.

The proper Golden coat requires very little grooming to look attractive. The density and correct length make it ideal in any conditions a hunting dog might encounter. Incorrect coats are not suitable in working conditions, as they do not provide the protection a dog needs and are more difficult to care for.

This Golden appears to have a nice front from this angle, with nice straight legs and good bone. (Janis Teichman)

COLOR: Rich, lustrous golden of various shades. Feathering may be lighter than rest of coat. With the exception of graying or whitening of face or body due to age, any white marking, other than a few white hairs on the chest, should be penalized according to its extent. Allowable light shadings are not to be confused with white markings. Predominant body color which is either extremely pale or extremely dark is undesirable. Some latitude should be given to the light puppy whose coloring shows promise of deepening with maturity.

Three shades of Golden colors. All are correct according to the breed standard. (Susan Kluesner)

Any noticeable area of black or other off-color hair is a serious fault.

Many people are not aware of the various shades of gold found among Goldens. Newcomers to the breed do not recognize the darker colored dogs as Goldens. Twenty-five years ago the dark golden color was the more common shade. Only popularity has made the lighter colors more prevalent.

Either end of the spectrum is correct, and a dog's working ability is not affected by the color of its coat. However, most hunters seem to prefer darker dogs, as they blend into the environment better. Dirt and mud is not as obvious on a darker coat, and the dog can be much dirtier and remain fairly attractive.

White spots on various parts of the body are quite common, especially in working lines. White on the feet, muzzle and forehead in addition to the chest are the areas most frequently marked. The presence of such white markings will not in any way affect the working abilities of the dog. In fact, part of the reason why white markings are so prevalent is because many of the best working retrievers have them, and consequently produce them. But white in any location other than the chest is not in keeping with the type and look described by the standard.

GAIT: When trotting, gait is free, smooth, powerful and well coordinated, showing good reach. Viewed from any position, legs turn neither in nor out, nor do feet cross or interfere with each other. As speed increases, feet tend to converge towards center line of balance. It is recommended that dogs be shown on a loose lead to reflect true gait.

The gait and overall structure are interrelated. A balanced dog that is properly constructed should move in a pleasing manner. Good movement is required to retrieve, quarter, swim effectively and perform all of the tasks of a working retriever.

TEMPERAMENT: Friendly, reliable, and trustworthy. Quarrelsomeness or hostility towards other dogs or people in normal situations, or an unwarranted show of timidity or nervousness, is not in keeping with Golden Retriever character. Such actions should be penalized according to their significance.

The outstanding temperament associated with the breed is one of the main reasons why many choose to obtain a Golden Retriever. A solid, typical temperament is more important in the makeup and relationship of a dog to the breed standard than any other feature.

Good structure makes for stylish movement on a water retrieve. (Jim Drager)

Disqualifications

Deviation in height of more than one inch from the standard either way.

Undershot or overshot bite.

MAKING SENSE OF IT ALL

Some aspects of the standard are easy to comprehend and relate to one's dog. It is easy to measure height and weight, determine pigment, bites and the presence of white hair. Angulation, overall balance and movement require an educated eye.

Before attempting to compare your dog to the standard, it may be a good

The Golden is a sturdy, athletic dog. The overall appearance is more important when assessing the dog than any individual feature. (American Kennel Club)

idea to ask for an evaluation from several people with experience. The more opinions, the better, as even experts differ in their ideas and interpretations. Remember, the standard is a written description of a visual image. That leaves plenty of room for interpretation.

Every dog has good points, and even the best have faults, though they may not be obvious to most eyes. The overall look and type of the Golden is of primary importance. It should be attractive, alert and radiate a joy in life that is reflected in a body that looks as if it could work all day and be ready for more the next day.

(June Smith)

CHAPTER 4

How to Find the Right Golden Retriever

Once you've made the decision to add a Golden Retriever to your life, the next step is to find one. This can be simple or very involved, depending on the criteria you have set. When contemplating Golden ownership, keep in mind some guidelines to help you make the best choices about what to look for and where to find a puppy.

THE IMPORTANCE OF AKC REGISTRATION

You will want to look for a puppy from an AKC-registered litter. However, bear in mind that this is not a guarantee of quality or good health. AKC-registered dogs are merely that—purebred and registered with the American Kennel Club. The AKC has no jurisdiction over the quality of animals bred.

So why look for AKC registration? It is your guarantee that the puppy is indeed a Golden Retriever and that the breeder keeps careful records of all their breedings.

When it comes to quality, headway has been made in the last few years. The AKC now notes hip and eye certifications for the parents on a dog's registration slip. As of January 1996, these clearances are only noted if dogs are positively identified by tattoo, microchip or DNA test at the time of examination. This is a positive step in a growing attempt to ensure honesty and soundness in breeding.

In many instances, real soundness and quality is a different matter entirely. This must be assessed by asking questions and taking it upon yourself to learn as much about the breed as possible to ascertain quality.

Regardless of why you want your Golden, it should be AKC-registered and from the best background of genetic soundness and intelligence. (Joanne Gaulke)

HIP AND EYE CLEARANCES

The first and most important criteria, regardless of any other goals, is to find a puppy from sound and healthy parents. This means that the sire and dam must have several health clearances. Look for breeders that advertise their stock as OFA/CERF.

OFA is the abbreviation for the Orthopedic Foundation for Animals. This organization reads and certifies hip and elbow X-rays sent in from veterinarians. Readings can be done at any age after six months, but clearance certification can only be done if a dog is 24 months of age or older. The OFA then rates the dog's hips as excellent, good, fair or a grade of dysplasia. These ratings are based on how tightly the ball and socket joint appear to fit and evidence of any wearing or irregularities of the bone surfaces themselves. Dogs with passing hips receive a certificate with a number and the rating. For example, the number might be 99999. This means it is the 99,999th Golden

Retriever to be issued a number. This is followed by the rating F, G or E. Then the dog's age in months is included, followed by the sex, F or M. If a dog is tattooed, a T will be added at the end. So the entire number will look like this: OFA GR 99999E24M-T.

A dog's hip rating is only valid for that dog. It does not indicate anything about the hips of the dog's parents, its siblings or what the dog itself will produce if bred. Life would be so simple if this were not true. The transmission of hip dysplasia is yet to be fully understood, but is believed to be polygenic in nature, meaning many genes are responsible. The environment may also play a role in whether hip dysplasia develops. Nonetheless, dogs with passing hips have a much greater incidence of producing offspring that are free of hip dysplasia. Any Golden bred should have OFA-certified hips.

Another organization that evaluates hips, and is becoming more frequently used, is PennHIP. Some breeders choose to use PennHIP evaluations rather than OFA, and many will have both evaluations. Rather than looking at an X-ray picture, as OFA does, PennHIP looks at the flexibility of the hip socket through measurements. Numbers are given that rate dogs within the norm for their breed.

Another soundness concern for Goldens is their eyes. The most common problem is cataracts of various types, which may develop at an early age or appear as a dog ages. There are other less common eye problems in Goldens, such as central progressive retinal atrophy (CPRA) and retinal dysplasia. Eyes are examined by board certified canine ophthalmologists and their reports are sent to CERF, the Canine Eye Registration Foundation. The exam forms are evaluated and a certificate and number is issued to a dog with eyes free of genetic disorders. A CERF number will indicate that this is the 99,999th Golden to receive a CERF number, followed by the year the exam was given and the age in months of the dog, like this: CERF GR 99999/97-24.

A common misconception is that permanent eye clearances are given after the age of eight in Goldens. This is true in Britain, but not in this country. Eye exams and CERF numbers can be given at any age, but they are considered to be valid for only one year. That means when you look at a CERF certification, it should not be more than a year old.

Testing hips and eyes has been commonplace for Goldens for three decades. During the last few years, increased research has indicated the importance of heart exams, thyroid screens and elbow X-rays, as well. Heart exams are particularly crucial because they are a matter of life and death. Goldens are susceptible to a genetic malformation of the heart known as subaortic articular stenosis, SAS. It manifests itself as a heart murmur of several grades, from mild to severe. A dog with any level of SAS should never be bred.

Heart exams are performed by board certified cardiologists. The owner should have a report of the exam. Additionally, OFA now certifies heart exams and issues a certificate and number. The number issued by OFA would have a CA to indicate the heart, with the number the dog is in relation to all Goldens with numbers, the age in months and sex, followed by a C. The entire picture would be OFA GR-CA000/23F/C.

What this all means is that when you are looking for a sound and healthy puppy, look for a litter where the sire and dam have OFA certificates for the hips and heart, and CERF certificates for the eyes. Hopefully, the presence of clearances is more than one generation deep and extends to the littermates of the dogs being bred, the grandparents, great-grandparents and even beyond.

But health and soundness is more than just clearances. Golden Retrievers are often known for skin problems, and the dogs in question should be

Quapaw's Royal Lukas of Britt, UD, enjoys a perfect life as a beloved companion and working obedience dog. (Terry Hanley)

trouble free with no apparent allergies or susceptibility to hot spots. Prospective buyers should question such things as overall health of the dogs and how long ancestors in the first two or three generations have lived. These are important questions that may have a significant bearing on the quality of life for your dog.

THE RIGHT GOLDEN FOR YOU

Once your health criteria have been set, you need to consider what you plan to do with your dog. If you are looking solely for a companion, you need not look for a show quality puppy or expect a breeder to sell you a top competition prospect. Anyone interested in an extremely active dog that can go all day may want to look for a puppy from more of a working background, where dogs close up in the pedigree have been used in field or obedience.

Anyone looking for a hunting or field dog should look for a puppy from a breeder that emphasizes retrieving skills. (Barbara Taylor)

Those with a more quiet lifestyle would do best by looking at a litter where the parents are of excellent quality and trainability, yet less demanding in their activity level. The best guide is always the parents; like begets like.

*Like begets like. Three generations of Goldens are pictured. In the middle is the grandfather, Ch. Wingwatcher Reddi to Rally, CDX, WC, (OS). On the left is his son, Ch. Elysian Sky Hi Dubl Exposure, UDT, MH**, WCX, (OS), and on the right is his granddaughter, Jetoca Magicgold Air Wings, CD, JH, WCX. (Cheryl Baca)*

Once your standards and goals have been set, you need to find a good breeder. There are several different kinds of breeders, and it's helpful to understand how they differ. Large kennel operations often have several breeds of dogs and produce many litters yearly in kennel facilities. The animals are usually well bred and have proper health clearances, although they are often untitled and do not receive the individual attention a smaller breeder offers. Puppies are sold on a business basis with little personal interaction between breeder and buyer.

Hobby breeders generally have only a few dogs and are often active in some type of dog competition. They will most likely be a member of the Golden Retriever Club of America, a local breed club or both. They may produce up to a couple of litters a year, though some only breed once every two or three years. This type of breeder has a serious interest in the placement of every puppy born. The sire and dam are often titled and will have health clearances. Puppies are usually raised in the house or in small kennel facilities.

The hobby breeder is usually active in some facet of competition, and strives to breed a Golden that fits the standard and has proof of ability and soundness.

The backyard breeder is most easily described as someone with a pet bitch who breeds because it would be fun to have a litter. Health clearances may be lacking, and the quality of the animals bred may be questionable. Backyard breeders produce the largest percentage of the Golden Retriever population.

Dogs and puppies can also be found through rescue groups and humane societies, and if you are simply looking for a pet, this can be a good choice for you. Rescued dogs come in all ages, sizes and both sexes. They are all unwanted. Many are sweet and humbly bred, with no fault other than that they no longer fit into their owner's life. Most of these Goldens make perfect pets for someone willing to give them a second chance.

THE BEST SOURCE

Rescue aside, the best place to obtain a puppy is from the serious hobby breeder. The best breeders carefully plan every litter to enhance the health and quality of the breed. Many also offer advice and support for the life of your dog.

Most people who become involved in the sport of dogs had no original intention of doing anything other than getting a nice pet and taking it to obedience class. But ideas do change. The key for anyone is to obtain a puppy from the best possible background of trainability and soundness. Dogs that are tractable can usually do anything with proper training. These dogs and litters are usually in the hands of serious hobby breeders. The parents will most likely have titles, and definitely health clearances as proof of their quality, trainability and soundness.

If your inclination is to purchase a puppy that can pursue a show career, you should go to a breeder known to produce outstanding conformation

Bogie was obtained as a pet and went on to get his Junior Hunter and Working Certificate. (Liz Hogan)

prospects. It is important to remember that in such a popular breed, a dog with excellent conformation and breed quality may still prove to be a disappointment in the show ring. This phase of competition requires dogs that go beyond the breed standard in type, coat, substance and size to be successful.

Conversely, if you are looking specifically for a hunting dog, seek a breeder that emphasizes field ability in their breeding program.

FINDING A GOOD BREEDER

There are a number of ways to look for breeders. Your search can begin in the telephone book. Some breeders or breeder-groomers are listed in the Dog or Kennel section. These people are usually involved with dogs or know others who are, and may offer referrals. Many times dog clubs or trainers will be listed; they, too, will often know of reliable breeders with litters.

Nationally published dogs magazines such as *Dog World*, *Dog Fancy* and the *AKC Gazette* usually have breeder listings. If you are looking for a hunting dog, *Gun Dog Magazine* and *Retriever Field Trial News* have extensive lists of litters.

The Internet has become a tremendous resource for anyone interested in dogs, and also has litter listings. You should not rule out local newspapers entirely, even though most ads listed here are not suitable. Phrases found in these ads, such as "champion lines," should be ignored, as the champions may be six generations back in the pedigree. But occasionally some fine litters are listed locally. Just check carefully.

Litters can also be located by contacting the Golden Retriever Club of America or a local Golden Retriever club. The American Kennel Club also has a referral number to assist potential buyers in finding a reputable breeder. This number is listed in Appendix A.

THE INTERVIEW

The first contact you make with a breeder is almost always by telephone. This initial conversation is actually an interview and is a good way for each of you to screen the other. While a potential buyer will have many questions, a good breeder will want to know as much about the buyer as possible. It is best to be prepared with a list of what you are looking for and your purpose for acquiring a Golden. The breeder will want to know about your family, job situation, house and yard, and any prior experience you may have had with dogs.

You should ask about field and show titles in the pedigree, health clearances and the breeder's involvement in the sport of dogs.

THE FIRST VISIT

If this first contact went well, you can schedule a time to look at the puppies. Most breeders do not allow anyone to visit a litter until they are four or five weeks old and have had their preliminary inoculations. If you are looking at several litters, be courteous and space your visits over several days rather than going from one litter to another. This is to prevent the spread of infection.

The premises the puppies are kept in, whether it is a whelping box, dog run or yard, should look clean and smell clean. Do not expect an immaculate house, as dog people are usually too busy with their dogs and puppies to clean their own home!

Ask to see the dam of the pups and any other related dogs the breeder may have on the premises. You can ask to see the sire, but many breeders do not own the sire, and he may live quite far away. Often photographs will have to suffice. Needless to say, the dogs should appear to be in good health. The dam should be in good weight, though her mammary equipment will be enlarged as she may still be nursing the puppies. She should be friendly, alert and more than willing to let visitors see her babies.

The dam should be in good weight and coat, though her teats may still be quite noticeable. (Janis Teichman)

The breeder should have health clearances available for the adults. Be sure to look for certificates with OFA and CERF on them. A four- or five-generation pedigree should also be available for both the sire and dam. The breeder may already have a litter pedigree available with both the sire and dam and their ancestors in their proper spaces.

The AKC registration papers may or may not be available, depending on the promptness of the breeder and the AKC in completing the paperwork. The AKC registration slips of the sire and dam may be present. Remember, dogs will not have health clearance certificates from OFA or CERF unless they are AKC-registered.

Golden Retriever puppies are cute, but not really much more than that until nearly five weeks of age. At this time they become extremely active and playful. It is impossible for a stranger to determine anything about potential adult traits at this stage. What you can determine is coat color, alertness and overall health.

It is not fair to you or the pups to expect to pick out a puppy at this time. A responsible breeder does not let a puppy go to a new home until it is 49 days old, and some may even hold on to their puppies for an additional week. In many cases, many of the puppies are reserved well in advance and only a few are available.

CONTRACTS AND REGISTRATION

Many breeders sell their puppies with contracts that outline what the breeder guarantees and the responsibilities of the buyer. There are many types of contracts, but a typical sample can be found on the next page.

Puppies that appear to be of competition or breeding quality may only be available on a co-ownership contract with the breeder. A separate contract will detail this partnership.

Puppies sold solely as pets should be available with AKC papers but with the Limited Registration restriction. This allows the dog to be registered and compete in all phases of dog events except conformation. However, this registration can be changed to full registration at a later date, with the approval and signature of the breeder. Dogs with Limited Registrations should not be bred, and if they are, the offspring are not able to be registered.

Many breeders do not believe in these attachments and sell their puppies outright. It is important for you to know in advance how the breeder intends to deal with registration and ownership.

Read the contract carefully. It may appear to say a lot, but actually promise nothing. It is doubtful that such a contract is ever binding, but it does indicate the intention of goodwill and standing behind what one breeds and sells.

Many breeders guarantee the health of the puppy for a 10-day period after it leaves their premises. They may go further and guarantee their puppies to be free of hip dysplasia and genetic eye problems and offer a refund or replacement puppy if the dog in question has never been bred and is neutered. Other breeders believe that they have done the best they can to ensure sound puppies by breeding healthy individuals and offer no guarantees at all.

The breeder may require a buyer to provide a completely secure yard, take the puppy through obedience lessons and contact the breeder first if placement of the dog becomes necessary. The good

Visiting a litter is fun for everyone. Some breeders will allow the buyer to select from several puppies. (Jeanine Campbell)

CONTRACT OF PUPPY SALE AND GUARANTEE

This is to certify that the male/female puppy sold to _____ on _____ has AKC litter number _____. The sire is Golden Glen Spencer For Hire SH, and the dam is Malcairn Miss Firequacker SH. Purchase price of this puppy is _____. This puppy is described as follows:

_____ Buyers have full ownership of this puppy.

_____ This puppy is sold on a co-ownership with the breeder. Please see additional contract.

_____ This puppy is sold on a limited registration. Full registration status may/may not be obtained at a later date when neutered or when OFA/CERF clearances are obtained.

BREEDER'S GUARANTEE:

All puppies may carry a 10 day health guarantee. If during that period the puppy becomes seriously ill and a veterinarian can attribute that illness to us we will refund the purchase price of the puppy.

A complete refund or replacement puppy is offered for any of the following defects:

1) crippling hip dysplasia requiring surgery or euthanasia
2) eye problems causing blindness
3) disabling problems of genetic origin
Written documentation is required from two qualified veterinarians or veterinary ophthalmologists.

For lesser problems that should in no way affect the working ability of the dog:

1) mild/moderate hip dysplasia from OFA reading no later than 28 months
2) non-affecting, but non-certifiable eye problems, no later than 28 months
We offer a replacement pup or a refund of 1/2 the original purchase price of the pup. This is valid only if the owner has made a serious effort to train the dog. We must receive copies of OFA or eye exam forms. Any replacements or refunds are only made on the condition that the dog covered by this contract has been spayed/neutered and we receive a veterinary certificate of verification. If this animal has been bred this contract is null and void.

BUYER'S RESPONSIBILITIES:

The buyer agrees to accept the duties of a responsible dog owner. These include, but are not restricted to 1) a completely fenced yard or dog run, 2) proper diet and veterinary care and 3) obedience classes. A dog should never ride in the back of an open vehicle unless it is in a sturdy crate. If this dog has a soundness problem, is a poor representative of the breed or if the owner has not taken the time and effort to prove the dog's worth as a working dog it should not be bred. No dog should be bred with OFA/CERF or other clearances that may be deemed necessary. Any dog or bitch it is bred to should have the same clearances. *If the buyer can no longer keep this dog the breeder MUST be contacted first.*

Buyer's signature _____ Date _____

Address _____

Telephone _____

Breeder's signature _____ Date _____

breeder's first goal is always for the best future and welfare of their puppies.

If you believe you've found the right litter, the breeder will normally require a deposit to hold a puppy. Future visits may be scheduled before the appointed pick-up day. Be sure to let the breeder know exactly what you are looking for in a puppy. They may be able to accommodate your wishes as far as sex, coat color and size, but the best puppy for your situation may not be your obvious choice.

Some breeders allow buyers to select their own puppy, first come first served, or based on dates that deposits are received. But it is rare for the serious breeder to allow this sort of selection process.

GRADING A LITTER

As puppies approach seven weeks of age, many breeders try to sort them out in an attempt at the best placement possible. All puppies are evaluated as to how they conform to the breed standard. If there are any with obvious faults that would preclude breeding or showing, these are automatically scheduled for a good pet home. Such puppies may have bad bites, undescended testicles, malformed tails, splotches of white in locations other than the

Selecting a puppy from a well-bred litter is often best left to the breeder, who knows more about each puppy than the buyer. (Jeannie Nutting)

toes or chest, homely heads or poor pigmentation.

Selecting real show prospects is risky at best, but here the breeder is looking for a beautifully put together puppy that exudes tremendous presence. Show quality litters are often graded from top show pick to finishable quality, the latter meaning a dog with no obvious faults that can go into the ring.

PUPPY TESTING

Breeders attempting to produce working dogs for various forms of competition often put their puppies through a series of temperament tests to assess their personalities. The results may help a breeder select a puppy that is best suited for a first-time owner and trainer, rather than the puppy a more experienced trainer might desire. The temperament tests most commonly used are a combination of tests originally developed by animal behaviorists and Guide Dogs for the Blind. Tests have been adapted to select hunting dogs by adding bird wings or actual birds to the testing process.

While tests do differ, the same general procedures characterize all puppy tests. It is recommended that tests be given in a location that is unfamiliar to a puppy and free of distractions. Puppies will often test differently in places they are accustomed to, and distractions would obviously hinder any testing.

First, sociability is tested by placing the pup several feet away from a stranger, who then coaxes the puppy to come. A bold, outgoing puppy will come charging, tail up, and even jump up on the tester.

Observing a puppy's reactions to new situations can tell a lot about its personality. (Andrea Johnson)

Other puppies will come readily with their tail up and merely greet the stranger. The less confident pup may come slowly with its tail tucked. The puppy that does not come at all and just sits there or even runs away may be extremely shy if it is looking for a hiding place, or extremely independent and not interested in people.

The tester then gets up and walks away from the puppy, encouraging it to follow. The dominant, people-oriented pup will follow and even get under foot, its tail up. Many pups will follow for a while and then get distracted and start to explore. The puppy that does not follow and goes away is indicating its lack of interest and its independence.

The puppy is then laid on its back by the tester with a hand on the chest to keep it in place for 30 seconds. Nothing is said and the belly is never scratched or rubbed in comfort. The dominant puppy will struggle, cry and even try to bite to gain its freedom. Many puppies will struggle with periods of settling. An indication of a willing puppy that should be easy to train is one that lies on its back and is relaxed, even making eye contact. The puppy that lies frozen, averts its eyes and hides its tail is often fearful and very submissive.

The puppy is then released and the tester makes continuous stroking motions from the top of the head down the back. The forgiving puppy will stay by the tester and even cuddle up. A dominant puppy may try to climb up and lick or bite the tester's face. The average puppy goes away to explore after a period of this social dominance. The independent puppy will go away immediately.

The natural instinct to retrieve is considered to be an excellent indicator of a dog's willingness to work for humans. In Goldens it is a part of their genetic make-up. The puppy is shown a small, crumpled-up piece of white paper. The paper is then thrown a few feet in front of the puppy. The ideal result for a puppy of any breed, but especially a Golden Retriever, is to go to the paper, pick it up and return to the tester with the tail up. Some puppies will go through the process slowly. Some will go out, but return without the paper. An independent puppy may run away with the paper. There are also puppies that show no interest at all in going out or retrieving the paper.

Some breeders check for sound sensitivity by banging a pan and observing the pup's reaction. Do they pay attention and go on with what they are doing, or do they spook and look for a place to hide? A real indication of how the noise affected the puppy is to show the puppy a towel and shake it in front of the pup on the ground, thus encouraging the instinct to chase. Puppies that are really bothered by the noise will be further scared by the towel and look for somewhere else to go. The stable puppy will show some interest in the towel, and those with high prey drive will chase it enthusiastically.

Breeders of dogs used for hunting or field work will throw a bird wing for the puppies in addition to or instead of the crumpled paper. The puppy that picks up the wing as fast as it can is generally considered a good choice for the job.

Breeders interested in the birdiness and retrieving instincts of their puppies introduce them to birds early. (Andrea Johnson)

While puppy testing is not fool proof, it helps sort out the puppies at the extreme ends of the temperament spectrum. Many times results are mixed, giving no real definite picture. In such a case it may be best to test again at another place and time. At seven weeks of age the personalities of puppies are just beginning to develop, and they are still quite malleable. Still, puppy testing can indicate the general direction a puppy is heading, and you can then adjust your training to make that puppy become the dog you want it to become.

The testing also gives the breeder a good clue as to where to place puppies. An extremely dominant, independent puppy is usually not a good choice for a first-time dog owner. This type of dog, if it is very people oriented and likes to retrieve, makes a good dog for the serious trainer. The puppy that tests in the middle in all areas generally makes the ideal pet for most people. The puppy that tests as shy, submissive and afraid must be placed with the utmost caution. Many times such puppies can be brought around with proper socialization early in life. Such puppies should never be placed in homes with children, and do best with the owner with few demands and a quiet lifestyle.

THE BIG DAY

When the puppies are ready to go to their new homes, the breeder may have one particular puppy in mind for you, or have two or three they feel would be suitable that you can choose from. Ask about each puppy, how it did on the temperament test and how it compares to the breed standard.

One almost always feels a certain attraction towards a certain puppy, and if all other things are equal, that is the puppy for you.

Many breeders put together an information packet that should include a pedigree, copies of health clearances, any health puppy records, such as a worming record and the first puppy shots, articles or lists of books that might be helpful and a copy of the sales contract.

At the time of purchase you should get the blue AKC registration slip, signed by the breeder. The registration slip an AKC puppy is sold with has blank spaces where the choice of a name is entered. Once a registered name is selected, the slip must be sent to the AKC within a year. Late registration is subject to a considerable monetary fine.

What you choose to call your puppy day to day is always your decision. But the name registered with the AKC is the dog's official name and is unchangeable. If you bought your puppy from a breeder with a registered kennel name, they may require you to include that name in the dog's registered name.

A kennel name is used to distinguish one breeder's dogs and breeding program from anyone else's. Some breeders even select themes for litters, or use a particular letter of the alphabet to denote a particular breeding. For example, the puppies from the "A" litter of Golddog Kennels might be named Golddog's Amos, Golddog's Adam, Golddog's Anna and so on. If you bought Amos, you might want to add a name you've chosen as well—perhaps your street. Then he'd be registered as Golddog's Amos of Wood Lane.

If the breeder has no kennel name, or does not require it be used, the choice is entirely up to you. Make sure your dog's name is distinctive and that you will not regret your choice later. What may seem cute for a puppy may not be fitting for a large adult male.

Selecting a suitable AKC-registered name requires careful thought. It should befit your beautiful new companion into adulthood. (Janis Teichman)

THE LONG-DISTANCE PURCHASE

If you're looking for a good pet, chance are with a little patience you will be able to find one locally. But if you're looking for a dog of a particular breeding or a specific purpose, sometimes it is not possible to find the right puppy in your area, and it might be necessary to look elsewhere. This can mean all your shopping is done by telephone. The breeder should send the potential buyer photos, videos, copies of pedigrees and health clearances. References from other breeders, trainers and even those with dogs from the breeder should be given freely. At the same time, the long-distance breeder may want the same type of information from the buyer.

BEYOND PUPPIES

A seven-week-old puppy is not the best choice for everyone. Many times breeders have older puppies available. These may be puppies the breeders have held on to so they can take a longer look at them, or some they just haven't found the right home for. Sometimes they were kept as show prospects but turned out to have some minor flaw that makes them fine pets but no good for the ring. If they have been properly socialized there is no reason a juvenile will not bond to a new owner.

The real advantage is that much of the guesswork has been removed. An older puppy is a more realistic picture of the adult dog than a seven-week-old puppy. At five months of age they are closer to their adult size and looks. The energy level, temperament and overall soundness are also easier to evaluate.

Another consideration is the adult dog. Golden Retrievers have the distinction of being the most loyal, most loving companions you can own, yet that love and loyalty is transferred easily. Assuming there are no behavioral problems and the dog has been raised in a normal environment, an adult dog is often the perfect choice. They have outgrown the destructiveness of puppyhood and are usually calmer. They are generally house trained and may have received extensive training.

An adult dog may be a better choice, depending on your circumstances. (Elaine Maloit)

Another advantage is that most soundness problems, if they exist, should be evident. Many soundness problems may preclude a dog from competition or breeding, but do not rule out a completely normal life as a pet with proper management.

Adult dogs can be found from breeders, and may be available for various reasons. Most of them have nothing to do with the dog's potential to be a very wonderful pet. The same resources used for finding a puppy are helpful in the search for an adult dog.

RESCUE GOLDENS

Golden Retriever rescue organizations exist in almost all parts of the country. Golden Retrievers end up in rescue for a wide variety of reasons, most of them not the dog's fault at all. If you have room in your heart for a Golden who really needs a second chance, a rescue dog may be right for you.

The adoption fee is usually minimal and goes towards helping to run the organization. Almost all rescue organizations require that a rescued animal be spayed or neutered.

Rescue volunteers are as careful in placing their charges as responsible breeders. Consequently, these dogs are not available to anyone. A secure and reliable home is a strict requirement for anyone wishing to own a rescue Golden.

A LIFE WITHOUT GUARANTEES

It would be nice if all dogs had long happy and healthy lives. But breeding dogs is an art rather than a science, and regardless of the care taken to breed sound dogs, the reality is that breeders have no control over genes and can only make educated guesses in their breeding choices. The same may be said of a buyer's attempts to choose the right breeder and the right puppy, or a breeder's attempt to place every puppy in the best possible home. People make mistakes and things go wrong, despite all the certificates, guarantees and contracts in the world.

If you plan to obtain your Golden Retriever from a breeder, the reliability of the breeder you choose is crucial. A reliable breeder is there to offer advice when it is needed and to help when things go wrong. If all Golden Retriever breeders took complete responsibility for every puppy they produced, there would be no need for Golden Retriever rescue. On the other hand, if all Golden owners took the time to stay in touch with their dog's breeder, everyone would benefit. Especially the dogs.

(Janis Teichman)

CHAPTER 5

Living With a Golden Retriever

Living with a dog of any breed requires preparation. This is not only for the welfare and happiness of the dog, but for the protection of your home and sanity. This is especially true if the new family member is a seven-week-old Golden puppy. Some Goldens are easy to raise and require few precautions. Others can be a challenge. Almost anyone who has ever owned a dog should have a good idea of what to expect. The first-time dog owner may be in for a real surprise.

PREPARING FOR THE NEW PUPPY

The breeder of the litter should have given you some advice and recommendations *before* you actually bring your puppy home. Now it's time to make your plans. The first decisions are where the puppy will stay when no one is at home and where it will sleep at night. This may be the same location. Your foremost considerations should be the safety of the puppy and preventing destruction.

The natural curiosity of a puppy often leads it to trouble. For this reason, the area selected must be as safe and immune to destruction as possible. An area in the garage, a laundry room, or even the bathroom may be suitable locations. If you plan to put up a barrier, it must be at least three feet high and away from anything a puppy might climb up on.

Many puppies are masters of escape, especially when boredom or curiosity gets the better of them. Leaving a young puppy in the backyard by itself is not a good idea. If a puppy is to be left outside alone for any period of time, it should be in an enclosed dog run.

Most Goldens are happiest if allowed to sleep somewhere indoors at night. They feel the security of being closer to their owner, are protected from the extremes of weather and the problem of nuisance barking is eliminated. If you're afraid your puppy might be destructive or soil the house at night, a dog crate will make life much simpler.

THE DOG CRATE

One of the most valuable and useful investments a dog owner can make is to purchase a dog crate. The crate simplifies house training and the decision of where to put the dog. Crates come in several varieties and sizes. The most versatile is the lightweight plastic crate that has a metal grated door and breaks down into two halves. It provides a secure place for the dog whether at home, in the car or in the back of a truck. This kind of crate is suitable for airline travel and can be cleaned.

The natural curiosity of puppies can get them into trouble. (Laurie Berman)

Puppies get into everything, even when they are outdoors. (June Smith)

A crate provides a secure place for a dog when it travels, especially in a truck. (Cheryl Baca)

Some people prefer crates made of metal wire. The advantage of these is that they provide more ventilation, stay cleaner and are completely collapsible. Their disadvantage is that they do not hold in the warmth in colder weather and are not suitable for airline travel.

Crates made of stainless steel or aluminum sheeting are extremely attractive and secure. These are more difficult to clean, heavier, do not break down and are much more expensive than their plastic counterparts.

The crate that an adult Golden would use is much too large for a puppy. Inexpensive, small crates can be purchased that are ideal for puppies under 12 weeks of age. When your pup has outgrown it, a small crate makes a great garage sale item, or it can be used for the family cat.

The correct size crate for an adult Golden depends the dog's size. A medium size crate is fine for a smaller Golden. The largest size may be necessary for a large dog. The dog must be able to completely stand up and turn around in the crate, or it is too small.

Some breeders will have begun crate training as early as six weeks of age by leaving a crate in the puppy enclosure. However, for most puppies, a crate is a completely new and unpleasant experience, but there are many things you can do to make it more positive. It helps if your outlook is that this is the best and safest place for a puppy. Start by feeding the puppy in its crate. At intervals throughout the day place the puppy in the crate with something it likes to chew or play with. A good time to do this is when you're busy with other things or need to run a short errand.

Many puppies will bark furiously, demanding their freedom, when placed in a crate, even if they

This young owner is prepared for the challenges of raising a puppy. (Jeanine Campbell)

Some breeders introduce their puppies to the crate by incorporating it as a part of their area. (Andrea Johnson)

are placed in there with food. If you are sure the puppy does not have to go to the bathroom, this is an opportune time for a puppy to learn to stay in a crate, and also to be quiet. Initially, give a quick rap on the crate along with a "quiet" command. If the barking persists, the crate should be placed in an area that is removed from the rest of the house, preferably behind a closed door. When the barking begins, open the door suddenly and command "quiet!" This is all some pups need.

The puppy can then learn to sleep in the crate at night. This is also an ideal way to house train, as a smart puppy learns quickly not to soil its sleeping area. If you are brave enough and willing to spend a few noisy nights, the crate can be kept fairly close by, or even in the bedroom. Quiet can be enforced with a quick rap on the top of the crate. Do remember, though, that persistent noise can mean the puppy really needs to relieve itself, and should be taken outdoors.

A crate makes an ideal, secure place for any dog to sleep at night, especially the young, the restless or the busy dog. But a puppy should never be left in a crate during the day for more than a few hours at a time. This is why it is so important for anyone who is away for long periods of time during the day to provide a proper environment for a puppy.

THE DOG RUN

A dog run may be the solution. You can purchase panels of chain link mesh attached to a metal framework, or design and construct a custom run. During the day most dogs, even puppies, spend the majority of their time lying around. Periods of activity are interspersed throughout the day and often require some sort of motivation. For this reason, the actual size of the run need not be large. You are not providing an exercise area, but rather a secure location for the dog to stay when you are away. A four foot by eight foot area is sufficient. An area no more than 10 feet by 10 feet is nice, but not necessary.

Dogs that are primarily kept in kennels and only come out for training or rare visits are customarily provided with long, narrow runs to provide exercise space. These may be up to 20 feet long and five feet wide. This is not how the Golden works, and such excess length is only a waste of space. The run should never take the place of a fenced yard, or of exercise time for your dog.

The sides of the run should be constructed of some type of wire mesh. Chain link is ideal, although any heavy, narrow gauged fencing material that the puppy cannot climb works well.

If the run is completely covered, the fence can be as low as six feet. In any case, the run should always be covered either by additional fencing material or a roof. This will prevent a dog from jumping or climbing out and offers protection from the sun and rain. A cement floor is the easiest to maintain, but may not be feasible. Other floorings that work are flat cement blocks laid side to side. This is more difficult to keep clean, but is easier to move if the location of the run is changed. Whatever flooring you choose, make sure it can't be dug up. Laying wire mesh underneath may help.

A run should have some type of a house for the dog, especially if it does not have a roof for protection from the elements. The house could be wooden or one of the many plastic pet houses available. An old plastic crate with the door removed also works well. In all honesty, some dogs never go in such an enclosure, but it's nice to give them the choice. At the very least, every run needs

Digging is a favorite pastime of almost all Golden puppies and dogs. (Janis Teichman)

a raised platform for the dog to lie on to get off the cold flooring material.

DOGS IN THE YARD

Whenever your dog is outside unattended, it should at least be in a fenced environment. The perimeters of the yard should be checked periodically for holes or weaknesses. A puppy can escape from an area that is secure for a larger dog. Before bringing home a puppy, the yard should be checked for any small openings in the fence.

Electronic dog fences are becoming increasingly popular. The way these work is that a wire is buried underground around the area of containment. The dog then wears a collar that emits electrical stimulation if the dog goes near the boundary.

This seems like a neat solution, but there are some drawbacks. The first is the cost and labor involved in digging the perimeter. Also, while this system will keep a dog within the confines of its property, it will not keep anything not wearing a collar from entering the area. This means neighborhood dogs and wild animals are free to enter at will.

A yard might even include a pool, especially in warm weather. (Cheryl Baca)

PROOFING THE HOUSE

Anyone who has had small children should understand the importance of removing anything harmful that might be within the reach of a toddler. The exact same thing applies to a puppy. Puppies are not only attracted to anything that might be at their level, but also anything that is within their reach if they jump or stand on their hind legs.

Small objects they might swallow and choke on should be removed. Electrical cords that might be chewed should be hidden. Anything of value that can be broken or chewed should be placed well out of reach. And that area of "reach" will increase quickly as a puppy grows.

House-cleaning materials, antifreeze for the car and any poisons should be placed completely out of reach. Plants that are both indoors and outdoors are another consideration, since some common plants are poisonous. Diffenbachia or dumbcane is a good example. The plant cells contain oxalic crystals that cause swelling of the mouth regions and possible death if any part of the plant is chewed.

KEEPING A YOUNG MOUTH HAPPY

All of these preparations and precautions are necessary not just for the sake of your property, but because a puppy enjoys oral exploration. Satisfying and curbing this trait can be done initially by providing a puppy with its own objects to play with, chew on and retrieve. There are countless toys and chewing devices on the market designed to appeal to the eye of the buyer and mouth of the dog. There are ropes in various configurations, plush toys, rubber squeaky toys and balls, just to mention a few of the items available.

Puppies need to chew and will use whatever they can find. (Susan Hutchinson)

Many toys are quickly destroyed, so the tougher and more durable the object, the better. Some puppies are satisfied with a Nylabone, especially if it is meat scented. However, the chewable Nylabones are very appealing and do not last for more than a couple of days when the dog gets older. These are extremely expensive for an adult dog, as the toy has such a short life span.

Puppies need their own toys to chew on. (Don Stevens)

Pig's ears will provide approximately an hour of enjoyment for a puppy, and increasingly less time as the pup's mouth and teeth become larger and stronger. A pig's ear is only a few tasty, expensive bites for an adult dog. Cow and horse hooves last considerably longer, giving many hours of pleasure to a puppy. As the piece becomes smaller it must be thrown away to prevent choking. The greatest drawback to these is the odor associated with them. The room will actually smell like a barn!

Rawhide chews are plentiful but have fallen into disfavor because the pieces are often bitten off and swallowed without being chewed. These will then swell up in the stomach and cause indigestion. A greater danger exists for the dog who tries to swallow large, softened chunks that can become lodged in the throat. It is quite possible for a dog to choke to death on a piece of rawhide.

The best chew for any price is a large knuckle bone. These can be purchased from butchers or at pet supply stores, and are sold smoked or plain. These provide weeks of chewing pleasure for puppies and adult dogs. As the bone becomes increasingly worn, watch for small broken-off pieces.

Some chewing items are safe to leave a dog with when you are away, such as a large Nylabone or new, large knuckle bone. Some of the other items mentioned should only be given to a puppy or dog when you are there to supervise.

A dog with too many toys may have a difficult time discerning what is theirs and what is yours. It is best to limit a puppy's toys and chewing objects to a select few. Just like a child who finds the greatest pleasure in sticks and rocks, a puppy will delight in a broken branch or piece of wood it finds. Sometimes the simplest items are the best, as long as they are safe. Teaching a pup to distinguish between objects that can be chewed and those that are off limits can be done with the aid of a spray such as Bitter Apple. This has an unpleasant taste and discourages chewing.

IDENTIFICATION AND CLOTHING

All puppies should wear a collar that should be fitted as soon as the puppy comes to its new home. This is the only piece of clothing a Golden will wear all the time. The best type of collar for a young puppy is made of a flat, narrow piece of webbed nylon. It can be a buckle style or have a snap enclosure.

This first collar will generally be adjustable to 14 inches. As a puppy approaches four months of age it will need a larger, adjustable collar. Depending on the adult size, another collar may be necessary later on. Once a dog has reached adult proportions you may wish to indulge in a leather collar.

Collars not only provide a means of identification, they also act as a handle. A puppy or dog can be held, guided and controlled by simply holding on to the collar or attaching a leash.

For years, attaching tags to a collar was the only means of identification available. Even though progress has created other ways of identifying your dogs, it is still a good idea to have some information on the collar. A metal or

Mike is ready for anything with a new collar and leash. (Janis Teichman)

plastic tag engraved with the owner's name and contact information still works, but such tags can easily fall off and be lost. A flat piece of engraved metal that is grommeted to the collar is much more reliable. The best information to include on this is the owner's name and telephone number. It may not be advisable to include the name of the dog or your address. Some people even write the telephone number on the inside of the collar with an indelible marker. This is not a good idea, though, because it can wear off or become covered with dirt over time.

The problem with collars is that they can come off, leaving a dog without any identification. One solution is to have the dog tattooed. This is best done on the lower abdominal area near the junction of a leg. Such areas often have less hair, and the tattoos are more easily read. The number can be the owner's Social Security number, the dog's AKC registration

Flare and Molly are dressed for Christmas, but they are also properly clothed with collars and identification tags. (Sally Jenkins)

number or a number provided by a national tattoo registry. Dogs are most commonly tattooed at veterinary clinics or tattoo clinics organized by breed clubs.

The use of microchips that are injected underneath the skin of a dog are becoming increasingly popular. The actual placement of the chip is quick and no more painful than a normal injection. A hand-held scanner detects the presence of a microchip, although it may not be able to read the code. As with a tattoo, a microchip number must be registered before it can be traced to you. The HomeAgain program registers all dogs with the

American Kennel Club. Another frequently used system is advertised under the name Avid. An 800 number is used to report lost or found animals.

Microchips and tattoos have become a useful tool in positively identifying dogs for hip and eye certifications as well. The AKC does not recognize clearances unless the dog is identified by microchip, tattoo or DNA test. It is best for dog owners to use several forms of identification: a collar for basic safety and a tattoo or microchip in case the collar is lost.

HOUSE TRAINING

With the housing, clothing and personal object issues tackled, you need to get down to the business of actually living with your puppy. The primary concern and the first step in developing the right relationship is house training. Success will be determined by how consistent you are day-to-day. There are some very simple rules to follow for the best and quickest results.

- Feed a puppy at the same time every day.

- Take a puppy outside to the same place after it has awakened, played for a period of time or just eaten.

- Praise the puppy after it has done its job.

- Confine the puppy when it cannot be watched or supervised.

- If the puppy messes in the house, never stick its nose in it, or physically reprimand it. A simple "no!" or a negative sound is sufficient.

A dog crate will make this task much easier, and is worth its cost for its convenience during house training alone. In real life, you'll use the crate as you apply the rules I have just listed.

If your puppy sleeps in a crate at night, you will immediately start the day by taking it outside to a designated location in the yard. Dogs quickly learn to associate the smell of the area with their duties. You may wish to do this on leash if the puppy is more inclined to explore. After finishing up, a play period may follow or free time in an enclosed part of the house. This might be the kitchen while you are preparing your breakfast.

After the puppy's morning meal it will again be taken outside to the same area. The remainder of the day will vary according to your lifestyle. Puppies quickly learn not to mess their crates, but it is not fair to leave a puppy there for long periods of time. You might alternate periods of crating with play time and free time in the yard.

When a puppy is in the house, you must learn to watch for the telltale signs that indicate the pup needs to relieve itself. The puppy might start sniffing strange places or become restless. The smart puppy might even go to the door. Learning to read these signs is important for success.

Goldens are often very quick to house train, and other than an occasional accident can be fairly reliable by three months of age.

ESTABLISHING A RELATIONSHIP

Every puppy needs some basic rules in order to fit into its new environment. If your relationship is to be successful, your pup needs to know its boundaries. All dogs are happiest when they have a leader. This is you, the person who makes decisions for them and makes the rules for them to follow. Some dogs have dominant tendencies; they naturally see themselves as superior to anyone or anything else. If puppy testing was done this may have been evident. If you chose a dominant puppy, be prepared for the battle ahead.

You begin establishing a sound relationship by placing the puppy on its back, as was done during puppy testing. The average puppy that struggles but quickly yields will need nothing other than praise when it settles and makes eye contact. Repeat this exercise several times during the early weeks.

This is also the perfect time to begin work with the puppy that is ceaseless in its struggles and even tries to bite. This type of reaction is not common in Golden puppies, but there are always

If you catch a puppy making a mess in the house, camly take it outside to finish up. (Andrea Johnson)

exceptions. With this puppy, grab the skin on the side of the neck and give the pup a light but firm shake while growling (you growl, not the dog). If done at an early age, this may be all that is needed to get this puppy under control and create respect. Older puppies that exhibit any aggressive behavior can be treated in the same manner, but should be shaken even harder and lifted off the ground. This may sound harsh, but is done only for the best interest and future of the dog.

Another exercise that is often neglected, but is equally important in building a relationship, is touching the puppies in places you may not normally touch. Begin by touching the paws and feet. Many puppies consider this to be a violation of their body and will make a real fuss. Touch each toe and even the nails. This will be important when you need to clip nails. Look in the ears and then look in the mouth. Lift the lips and then spread open the jaws. The puppy must know that you are in complete control. It's also important to be able to handle your dog this way if you suspect it has an illness or injury.

Establishing a leader relationship is important for everyone in the household. This may be difficult if you have children, because dogs tend to see them as equals rather than leaders. This becomes especially evident with mouthiness problems. Puppies are frequently accused of biting children, when the fact is that as far as the puppy is concerned, it is only playing with a littermate in typical puppy fashion—which includes nipping. This may be a difficult point to get through to your children and to your dog. Children like to play using their hands as a toy, but should not be allowed to play with a puppy that way. Pups should *never* get the idea that a hand is something to nip at.

The key to avoiding the problem begins with your own reaction. Chewing on an adult's ankles or arms can be dealt with in several ways. Initially a quick "no!" and a jerk away from the puppy can be enough to deter the milder pup from continuing. You simply have let them know they have gone too far. Spraying these areas of the body with Bitter Apple can also get the idea across to a puppy.

There are some key words or sounds that every puppy should need to learn. Start with a growling sound that is something like "aargh!" This can then be expanded to include "no," "off" and "quiet." These words can be used to help set your rules and enforce them. Consequently, when a puppy begins to chew on anything inappropriate, a quick verbal sound will remind the puppy it is doing something undesirable. The area can also be

A puppy quickly learns to lie at its owner's feet. (Joanne Gaulke)

Mother dogs establish their leadership by using signals and body language. Puppies understand this language and don't consider it harsh. (Andrea Johnson)

sprayed with Bitter Apple to curtail the desire to chew there.

LIFE'S BOUNDARIES

The boundaries you set for you puppy should be set for life. Do not allow your puppy to do anything you would not want your adult dog to do. If you do not want a dog to lie on the couch or sit in your lap or jump up on the table or beg for food, now is the time to teach these rules. It may be cute for a puppy to sit in your lap or beg, but it's not cute when an 85-pound hairy adult does the same thing.

Give the puppy its own bed in the corner of the dining room. Give it a favorite chew toy and teach it to stay there while the family eats. Move the bed next to the couch and the pup will learn to lie there while the family watches television.

If an infraction occurs, give a verbal correction, and follow this with something positive the dog can complete. With a really persistent problem, you can set up traps, such as empty cans falling down in a clatter or balloons bursting when the boundaries are violated. You can also buy mats that emit an electric charge to keep a dog off the couch.

QUIET AS A WAY OF LIFE

Most Goldens are quiet and only bark when necessary. The easiest way to teach an understanding of the word "quiet" is with a crate. When the crated puppy persists in barking (and the only reason is because it wants to be somewhere else), a verbal reminder to be quiet is given. When it continues, a shoe or anything else that makes a loud thud can be thrown at the side of the crate at the same time the "quiet" command is given. This must be a surprise in order to be effective. The puppy now has a clear idea of the meaning of "quiet" and how to prevent unpleasant surprises. Many barking problems could have been avoided if dealt with properly at a young age.

Some dogs bark due to separation anxiety. Leaving a radio on where the dog can hear it can alleviate this barking.

If there is no other way to control excessive barking, there are tools such as electronic bark collars that can eliminate stress to the owner, the neighborhood and, most important, the dog. Using electronic devices to train your dog is a serious step, so be sure to consult a professional dog trainer if this is the course you wish to follow.

There is nothing quite so relaxing as a nice nap. (Janis Teichman)

Freshly dug holes make perfect places to play. (Laurie Berman)

THE EARTH MOVER

Digging holes in the ground is one of a dog's great pleasures in life. Unfortunately, this destroys nice yards and lawns. The real culprit is usually a mole or gopher; dogs dig in an attempt to root out the varmint, and in the process make a real mess. Digging also gives a dog something to do and fills many idle hours for a bored dog.

Most of the so-called remedies designed to stop a dog from digging are failures. The most effective thing to do is to rid the yard of burrowing animals. The next is to give the dog something else to do and provide ample exercise.

Another idea is to provide an area that is solely for the dog, where it is free to dig to its heart's content.

THE BASIC COMMANDS

The basic obedience commands a dog will need throughout its life can be taught from the start.

Puppies respond especially well if small pieces of their food or pieces of hot dog are used to motivate and reward their behavior.

"Sit" means to sit and remain in one place until released. When this exercise is initially introduced, a piece of food is held directly in front of the pup's nose and slowly moved up and behind its head. As it moves its head back to follow the food, it automatically goes into the sit position. Initially the command is given as the action is completed, and then is gradually given earlier and earlier until it precedes the action.

"Down," which means to lie down (as opposed to getting off something), is taught in a similar

Nicole Campbell is ready for puppy training with her puppy, Timber. (Jeanine Campbell)

manner. The puppy is moved with food or placed in a sit position and the food is moved in a slow down and outward motion. When the puppy is completely down, the food is given.

The sit and down can be used as measures of control. The puppy should sit when approached and to be petted, rather than being allowed to jump all over a person.

Remember that if a puppy is given a command and it does not respond, the puppy should be made to comply without any further commands. Dogs learn to ignore your requests faster than they learn to obey. Puppies are only babies, and complete compliance to commands can never be expected. However, it can be enforced.

"Come" is the most important command any dog will learn. A leash will now be needed. The puppy can be called from person to person within the family, always with its name said first, followed by the verbal command "come." An encouraging tug on the leash in the correct direction may be needed. As the puppy approaches it should be given praise and a small treat.

Now take the puppy to places with distractions. Let the puppy go to the end of the leash and explore, then say its name and "come," give a quick tug, move backwards, then praise and reward. It is important never to call your dog to you for a scolding or correction. It will quickly associate the act of coming with a correction, and will be less and less likely to come when called.

Walking on leash with a puppy can be a real challenge, but any time a puppy is out of its house or yard it should be on leash. If a puppy constantly pulls, let it go out ahead, keep the leash as loose as possible and then make a quick about-turn. When the puppy feels the resistance and realizes the person on the other end of the leash is somewhere else, it will hurry to catch up. Give it a treat when it gets to you, and praise. Keep repeating this until the puppy gets the idea that the best thing to do is to walk somewhere close to you. Try to keep the leash loose, as dogs tend to pull more if the leash is tight.

A puppy that is hesitant about walking on leash can first be allowed to spend time in the house or yard with the leash attached to the collar but dragging freely, until it is comfortable. This should only be done under supervision, to make sure the

Teaching a puppy eye contact is important in establishing a relationship. This can initially be done in both the sit and down positions. Hold a small piece of food to your face near the eye and tell the puppy to "watch." When the puppy makes eye contact, give the reward. Gradually increase the period of time the puppy must watch before the food is given. (Janis Teichman)

leash does not snag on anything. When you take this pup on walks, encouragement and praise should be used rather that trying to pull the puppy forward and creating resentment.

PRE-SCHOOL AND BEYOND

All puppies and their owners can benefit from attending some type of obedience class. Most obedience clubs and private trainers offer classes designed for puppies 11 weeks and older. A puppy should not attend until it has completed the series of DHLP shots.

Puppy class provides an excellent means of socialization, as the puppy is exposed to a different environment and lots of other dogs. This is all important in the development of a normal dog. Besides the beginnings of basic obedience, the puppy may be introduced to a variety of new ideas. Some of these might include going over, under or through strange objects, retrieving and grooming instruction. Every class is different.

Obedience training does not end with puppy school. By the time a Golden Retriever is about six months old it is mentally and physically mature enough for real obedience training. Again, an obedience class is an excellent idea, as the dog will continue to be exposed to other dogs and people and learn to behave in different environments. A frequent comment one hears is that a dog does everything fine at home, so why should it need obedience. But what about when it is not home?

Bear in mind that obedience class is never an instant solution to a behavior problem. Almost all dog problems are rooted in a confused relationship as to who is actually in control. Obedience training is the only way to begin rectifying this situation, but the solution is long term.

All of the commands you have already learned will be taught and reinforced with a greater degree of control and perfection expected. A dog will eventually learn off-leash control as well.

A dog that successfully completes a basic obedience class (and it often takes several repetitions) is a pleasure to live with. Nothing makes a dog happier than knowing its correct behavior is pleasing its owner. This only strengthens the bond between dog and human. The respect and

Some puppy classes introduce puppies to a variety of new situations. This pup is coming through a tunnel. (Sandy Sproull)

admiration a dog gains for its owner through obedience will carry over to all facets of life.

THE SECRET IS ATTENTION AND EXERCISE

While obedience training will greatly improve your relationship with your dog, the time you spend with it is another important factor. During the hour or so you are at class, and the daily periods of time you spend in practice, your dog is the sole focus of your life. Dogs crave this type of one-on-one attention.

The attention is all important, whether you are attending a class or not, but so is the exercise they receive during training. Time and exercise are key ingredients to a dog's happiness. A body that receives regular exercise is more likely to be fit and healthy. Exercise is important in preventing boredom.

Being retrievers, Goldens can spend lots of time performing the act that is a part of their name. It can be a ball, a Frisbee, a stick or training

A well-adjusted, normal Golden is raised with proper care and common sense. (Janis Teichman)

bumpers. Swimming is another exercise many Goldens enjoy. Some have been known to do laps in the swimming pool on their own. The secret is that they want to enjoy life with you, and good behavior, obedience and proper exercise all lead to the best quality time possible for a Golden Retriever.

(*Janis Teichman*)

CHAPTER 6

Keeping Your Golden Healthy

G ood health is not just a matter of genetics. All dogs need veterinary care and preventive measures to ensure a healthy life. This includes regular vaccinations, parasite control and blood screens as a dog ages to make sure everything is functioning properly.

Your dog's breeder laid the groundwork for the dog's health by breeding the soundest dogs possible, in the hope of producing offspring free of genetic problems. They very likely will have wormed the puppies regularly, if necessary, kept the premises flea free, kept the dam well fed and healthy to produce nutrient-rich milk, and weaned the pups to a high-quality puppy food. Now you are responsible for all future care.

SELECTING A VETERINARIAN

Finding a veterinarian you feel comfortable with and confident about is essential to a good veterinarian-patient relationship. Try to select a veterinary clinic before you bring your puppy home. Many times the breeder will recommend their own veterinarian. If this is convenient, it may be ideal, as the clinic may already have some records of the puppies and the breeding program they came out of.

Another way to find a vet is to ask people who have animals for recommendations. Call dog-related businesses, such as groomers and boarding kennels, for suggestions. A consensus or many referrals to the same clinic is a good sign.

The foundation of a healthy future has been laid down by the dam and the breeder by providing a nutritious diet and proper care. (Andrea Johnson)

Next is to visit the clinic personally. Accessibility is an important factor, in case of emergencies. The parking area should appear clean, though a new building or fancy surroundings is not indicative of quality. A busy parking lot, friendly staff and good recommendations are the best signs.

THE FIRST VISIT

Many times a puppy has already received its first inoculation (the one given at seven weeks) before leaving the breeder's home. Some breeders have each puppy examined by their veterinarian before they leave. At this time the temperature is taken, and mouth, ears, eyes and skin are examined for any obvious problems. The heart is checked for murmurs and the testicles are checked in male puppies to see if they are present and have descended. A puppy that has received a shot at six

to seven weeks of age and has had a preliminary examination need not go to the veterinarian again until the second shot is given at 11 weeks of age. If the breeder has not given the shot, or has given the first shot themselves but no examination, then the puppy's first visit should be within the first day or two after leaving the breeder.

VACCINATIONS

The DHLP combination shot a puppy receives at seven and 11 weeks of age protects it from distemper, hepatitis, leptospirosis and parvovirus. A parainfluenza vaccine, which offers protection from some strains of kennel cough, can also be given at 11 weeks. A puppy should be kept confined to its own house and yard until after receiving the second DHLP shot. It is unwise to place a puppy in a situation where the possibility of disease exists until it is fully protected.

Most veterinarians recommend that a puppy continue to be given booster parvovirus and corona virus vaccinations every two weeks through four months of age. The reason is that the puppy carries natural immunity from its dam that gradually wears off. A vaccination given while that immunity is still active is blocked and is actually ineffective. Giving the shots through later weeks ensures the immunity from the shot itself will take effect.

The rabies vaccination is given at about four to five months of age. For the remainder of the

A puppy should see the veterinarian you have chosen within the first few days after you bring it home. (Janis Teichman)

dog's life the standard vaccination schedule has been a booster DHLP shot every year, parainfluenza or bordatella every six months and rabies every three years. New studies indicate that even DHLP vaccines need only be given every three years, so it is best to consult your veterinarian.

Certain aspects of vaccinations are in the spotlight these days. There are serious dog fanciers who do not believe in vaccinations of any kind. Their philosophy is that the antibodies injected are actually harmful to a dog and that many dogs become ill or die from vaccinations.

It is true that some breeds are more prone to problems. But in the real world, boarding kennels, groomers and reputable obedience classes require proof of vaccination for any type of service. The actual number of dogs that have a reaction to a vaccination is very small. It is better to vaccinate regularly and wisely rather than to risk a dog's health.

FLEAS

Fleas have coexisted with dogs since the beginning of time, and were once the bane of most dog owners. They were the source of constant scratching and chewing, which created skin problems and introduced tapeworms into a dog's internal system. They were everywhere our dogs were, and even on us. More money was spent on flea control and eradication and visits to the veterinarian for flea-related problems than probably any other health concern.

But the little pests may soon be on their way to extinction, thanks to three products on the market, only available through a veterinarian, that are safe, easy to use and deadly only to fleas. Program is a pill that is taken monthly and works by blocking the reproductive cycle of the female flea. Eggs

Dogs of all ages require regular vaccinations to prevent illness. (Janis Teichman)

If Program is used, it may be necessary to use another method of flea control to kill fleas that might get on the dog when it travels. Some veterinarians recommend using both Advantage and Program at the same time for total protection and elimination of the flea problem. But even using just one of these products often solves the average flea problem completely. And, depending on where they live, some people have found that once the fleas are eliminated, active flea control becomes unnecessary. However, it's wise to always be vigilant, because a dog can be reinfested by fleas brought by other dogs or found in other areas.

The old-fashioned methods of flea control still abound and should probably be mentioned. Sprays work for up to two weeks, killing any fleas on the dog and preventing new ones from jumping aboard. Flea dips work for the same duration and in the same manner. They must be applied to a freshly cleaned dog. Flea shampoos only kill the fleas that are on the dog and have no residual effect. The premises where the fleas live and breed should be sprayed with insecticides, and flea bombs can be used in the house.

MANGE

Cheyletiella mange is common on many dogs and produces a condition in young puppies known as walking dandruff. The presence of this large red

are laid, but they are sterile. No viable eggs, no new fleas, soon no fleas at all. Two other products, Advantage and Frontline, are liquid solutions placed on the dog's skin where the neck and back meet. On large dogs a spot is also placed on the back above the tail. The solution spreads over the dog's body. When a flea bites the dog, it is killed.

The liquid products should not be used on breeding animals, but have no other restrictions. Studies vary as to how long these products are effective, but both provide excellent control and continue to be effective even after a dog swims or is bathed. It is always important to read the directions and follow a veterinarian's advice when using any such product.

mite produces dandruff-like flakes that are found on the head, neck and back. There may be some mild scratching and the dandruff does not go away, despite grooming attempts.

The interesting thing is that when normal flea control measures are used, this mite is usually also contained. When flea control is no longer needed, or when a product specific only to fleas is used, this mite flourishes. Many adult dogs may have it and only scratch occasionally, with no signs of dandruff. It is only readily evident on puppies.

Diagnosis is made by actual identification of the mite under a magnifying glass or microscope. It is treated with shampoos, dips and sprays that list mites or lice as one of the parasites they can be used for.

Two other mites that cause disease are sarcoptic mange and demodectic mange. The first causes intense itching and scratching, because the mite that burrows into the dog's skin. It is treated by insecticide dips.

Demodectic mange is caused by a mite that lives in the skin pores of all dogs. The mite takes control during periods of stress or when the natural immune system is weakened. It is most commonly seen in dogs three to 12 months of age and is characterized by hair loss without itching. Diagnosis and treatment should be done with veterinary supervision.

TICKS

Ticks are common in many parts of the country and are the cause of several serious diseases. Lyme disease is the one of most concern, as it has spread

Dogs worked outdoors are more likely to pick up ticks. Tick prevention measures may be necessary, along with checking for ticks after training sessions. (Susie Rezy)

nationwide. It is transmitted to the dog when it is bitten by tiny, infected deer ticks. If one lives in an area where this is known to be a problem, or if a dog is exercised or trained in an area infested with ticks, it is advisable to prevent the problem. There is a tick vaccination on the market, as well as tick collars and sprays. Frontline, mentioned earlier under flea control, has also been shown to provide some protection from ticks.

Whenever a dog is in an area where ticks may be present, it is a good idea to comb it thoroughly. Ticks are often found on and around the head, as they gravitate there in the search for fluids.

Vaccinating a dog against Lyme disease is debatable. It may not be completely effective, and once a dog has been vaccinated it will test positive for the disease in the future.

Lyme disease exhibits itself in a number of ways. It may manifest itself initially as lameness, stiff joints and lack of coordination and fever. If untreated, it can lead to death. It is difficult to diagnose even with blood tests, and the symptoms mimic many other problems. A dog testing positive for the disease is placed on antibiotics and thereafter tested periodically. Lyme disease affects humans, too.

WORMS

At your puppy's first veterinary visit, bring along a fresh stool sample. As a dog matures, stool samples should be periodically checked. Unless it is possible to actually see worm segments in the stool, this is the only way the presence of worms of the intestinal tract can be confirmed.

Activities near the water are great, but there is an increased risk of mosquito bites around water. The protozoan, giardia, is also picked up by exposure to contaminated water. (Janis Teichman)

Roundworms (*Ascarids*) are the most common worms found in puppies. They pass from the dam to the puppy during pregnancy. They are easily removed and may have already been treated by the breeder. The roundworm has little effect on the adult dog, but in puppies it may cause poor weight gain, diarrhea and vomiting. Serious infestations left untreated can lead to death.

Tapeworms (*Cestodes*) live in the small intestines and look like grains of rice in the stool or around the dog's rectum. The tapeworm is carried by fleas and is passed to the dog when it swallows a flea. If fleas are on the outside, tapeworms are almost always in the inside.

It is best to be rid of these parasites, as they, too, can cause weight loss and a poor coat. The medication to eliminate tapeworms from the system is simple to give and works well, but if the flea problem is not addressed, the tapeworms will be right back.

Whipworms (*Trichuris vulpis*) and hookworms (*Ancylostoma*) are seen less frequently and are acquired primarily through contaminated soil. Whipworms are long and thin and attach themselves to the wall of the large intestine. They are responsible for diarrhea and weight loss. Hookworms are thin and short. They inhabit the small intestines and primarily affect young puppies. Weight loss, anemia and diarrhea are frequent signs. Diagnosis is made by the presence of eggs in the stool.

Protozoan Diseases

The most commonly seen diseases caused by these microscopic organisms are coccidiosis and giardia. Both cause loose stools that contain mucous and blood. In the case of coccidiosis, lethargy and loss of appetite quickly follow.

Both of these diseases can be difficult to diagnose because the organisms have a short life span outside of their host. Extremely fresh stool samples are necessary for identification.

Infection with giardia is usually through contaminated water. Coccidiosis flourishes in humid conditions where the area is filthy or difficult to clean. Puppies kept on damp ground that is infected with the spores (oocytes) are likely victims, while puppies kept on a surface that can be regularly cleaned and disinfected are usually safe.

Coccidiosis is transmitted when the oocytes, which may lie dormant in a contaminated area, are ingested either by eating soil or feces. It normally takes five to seven days from the time of ingestion to signs of illness. Both diseases are treated and eliminated fairly easily with specific drugs from a veterinarian.

Heartworm

The most dangerous internal parasite is heartworm (*Dirofilaria immitis*). As the common name suggests, the adult worm actually lives in the right side of the heart, though it can later travel to the lungs and liver. A dog is exposed when bitten by a mosquito carrying the larvae. These then enter the bloodstream, developing into microfilariae, which eventually enter the heart and mature into worms.

A dog may have heartworm for six months or more before any signs are seen. Usually the first signs are shortness of breath and a persistent deep, soft cough. Progressive symptoms are the same as those seen in congestive heart failure. Left untreated, a dog with heartworm will die.

Diagnosis is confirmed by a blood test that detects the microfilariae. However, for a variety of reasons, the microfilariae may not be present in the blood. If heartworm is suspected, further tests, such as X-rays and an electrocardiogram, may be needed to confirm the diagnosis. The reason for extreme caution in the diagnosis is that the actual treatment is radical, and many times the patient does not survive the medication itself.

Heartworm can be avoided by placing the dog on a preventive that is taken orally. In the past this was usually a small pill taken daily and marketed under several names. Now most people prefer a chewable tablet such as Heartguard that is given monthly.

Before beginning any heartworm preventive program, a dog must always be tested to make sure it is heartworm-free.

One word of warning: If you have no reason to suspect your dog has heartworm but it tests positive, have the dog tested again. It may even be advisable to go to another clinic for a second opinion. Diagnosing heartworm is not easy, and the treatment is dangerous.

Even if heartworm does not exist in your immediate area, placing your dog on a preventive is necessary if you travel with your dog.

Heartworm-carrying mosquitoes can breed in a pond just a few miles from where you live.

AN OUNCE OF PREVENTION

I hope it's becoming obvious that much of a dog's good health depends on prevention. Infectious diseases are controlled by vaccination and parasites by preventive applications and medications. Regular grooming and examinations are another easy way to prevent problems before they develop.

The rest is not so readily in our control. Most of the other problems your dog may be faced with are genetic in origin, or in a dog's predisposition to develop them.

STRUCTURAL PROBLEMS

A puppy may seem perfectly sound, but as it matures any joint and bone problems will become increasingly obvious. Puppies with serious hip or elbow dysplasia or osteochondritis may begin to exhibit signs when they're as young as five months of age.

Hip dysplasia is the malformation of the ball and socket joint of the hip. There are varying grades of dysplasia, from mild to severe. A severely affected dog may have almost no joint at all. A mildly affected dog may have hips that appear almost normal with minor irregularities.

Accompanying hip dysplasia is arthritis. The age at which the arthritis appears has a

large bearing on how the disease progresses. A dog with mild dysplasia but early arthritic changes may be more painfully affected than a moderately dysplastic dog with very little arthritic changes. Additionally, dogs vary in their pain thresholds, with some very dysplastic dogs leading fairly normal lives, while sensitive dogs may show great signs of pain with a much better pair of hips.

The first signs of a problem may be limping, lameness or difficulty in getting up after lying down. A young dog that tires quickly after even moderate exercise may be in pain.

Fortunately, dogs that have milder forms of the disease might never have visible signs and should lead normal lives. Their dysplasia does become a problem when breeding is concerned. Because this

A careful breeding program, where both parents are screened for genetic problems like dysplasia, ensures healthy dogs that are able to perform the traditional functions of the breed. (Sue Nelson)

is a genetic defect, dysplastic dogs should not be bred.

Hip dysplasia can only be confirmed by X-ray. Obvious cases can be detected by most veterinarians, but more subtle abnormalities may need a specialist's trained eye.

The prognosis for the future of a seriously dysplastic dog varies and depends on the amount of money one is willing to spend. Surgery to replace the hip socket is effective but expensive. Another common surgery severs the muscle and permits more laxity and movement. The choice is a personal one. Dogs that are in great pain may even be euthanized—never an easy decision, but sometimes a humane one.

Rapid bone growth can lead to problems in young dogs. Good genetics and sound parents are the best insurance for a puppy to grow up to be healthy and sound. (Jeannie Nutting)

early as six months of age. X-rays are used to diagnose the problem, and surgery usually corrects it.

The genetics of the inheritance of both types of dysplasia are complex. The disease is considered to be polygenic, which means more than one gene plays a role. The environment is often also blamed for dysplasia. Held to blame are slick floors, poor nutrition and excessive exercise. Unfortunately, even puppies raised in the best situations develop dysplasia. Through selective breeding, the incidence of severe hip dysplasia has declined over the years in lines produced by serious breeders. But it is only with continued diligence and by breeding dogs with sound hips that hip dysplasia can be controlled.

Dysplastic dogs should never be allowed to become overweight, as excess pounds can make a manageable problem severe. These dogs should be given regular periods of mild exercise, but never for long periods. Walks and swimming are ideal exercise for the dysplastic dog.

Elbow dysplasia is the incorrect union of the elbow joint. An affected dog will become lame as

Osteochondritis, or OCD, has become increasingly common in Golden Retrievers, and a genetic predisposition is suspected. This is a disease that primarily affects the growing bones of the shoulder, hock and stifles, causing improper formation of cartilage on the head of the long bone. Typically, a dog with OCD shows increasing lameness, though it may begin as a sudden occurrence set off by an injury. Some injuries are difficult to prevent, but many can be avoided by not allowing a young dog to jump from heights. The limping may appear to go away after periods of rest but quickly reappears with exercise.

Again, diagnosis must be done by X-ray. Because this is a problem the average veterinarian is often unfamiliar with, it may be necessary to go to a specialist, or at least a veterinarian with experience in treating OCD.

Sometimes with long periods of inactivity, OCD is outgrown. However, months of doing nothing at all are difficult for an active young dog. Surgery may be the best solution and is usually effective. Most dogs who have had OCD go on to lead normal lives, though the affected ones may always have a weak spot in their structure and be prone to injury.

Panosteitis is another bone disease that causes lameness in young dogs. Like OCD, it is usually associated with larger dogs experiencing rapid bone growth. The lameness is never specific and seems to move from limb to limb. There is no known treatment and the problem usually goes away on its own.

THE EYES

Serious problems that affect normal eyesight are rare in Goldens. Cataracts and central progressive retinal atrophy (CPRA) are of primary importance, but the average veterinarian would not notice or be able to diagnose them. If a dog appears to be disoriented, runs into things and lacks focus, an eye problem should be suspected.

Further confirmation should be done by a canine ophthalmologist.

A cataract is considered to be any type of opacity on the lens of the eye. There are many causes, with injury and diabetes being the most common. In some cases, cataract surgery is successful.

The two types of cataracts most commonly found in Golden Retrievers that are genetic in origin are juvenile cataracts and Y sutures. Diagnosis must be done by a specialist, and a dog with either type of cataract should not be bred.

More obvious to an owner is the dog with eyes that constantly tear or have drooping rims. The first problem is usually caused by either a blocked tear duct or eyelashes that grow inward, towards the eye's surface. The eyelash condition is known as distichiasis or trichiasis. Distichiasis is the presence of extra lashes that often grow in an atypical position. Trichiasis is the growth of eyelashes in an abnormal position, usually inward, towards the eye. Many times these conditions occur without any obvious abnormal tearing.

The incorrectly placed hairs can be removed if they are causing obvious discomfort to the dog. Blocked tear ducts are also corrected surgically.

Entropian is the condition in which the eyelid turns inward, causing irritation. The condition where eyelids turn outward and droop is called ectropian. Both conditions can be corrected by surgery. This procedure will improve the appearance of the dog and help prevent foreign objects from getting in the eyes—one of the functions of the properly positioned eyelid.

It is important to remember that such surgical corrections eliminate a dog from the conformation ring. Additionally, dogs with abnormal eyelids should not be bred. Distichiasis and trichiasis may require special consideration if breeding is contemplated. Any exams or surgeries should be performed by an eye specialist.

THE HEART

In the last 15 years it has been acknowledged that Golden Retrievers are prone to a genetic heart disorder. Certainly, heart problems always occurred randomly and older dogs died of heart failure, but a particular problem was beginning to show up regularly and with frightening genetic implications. The problem was eventually diagnosed as subvalvular aortic stenosis (SAS). In the past it was primarily associated with Newfoundlands, but more and more Goldens were dying suddenly, and autopsies indicated SAS.

SAS is the malformation and misfunction of the fibrous ring that is just below the aortic valve.

Dogs can be allergic to grass and pollen, just as humans are. (Janis Teichman)

This ring restricts the flow of blood to the body. The problem is diagnosed by careful listening with a stethoscope to see if a heart murmur typical of the disease is detected.

Murmurs are classified in four grades, I to IV, with I and II being very mild and quite difficult to detect. Serious murmurs are of grades III and IV and are easily detected. If a murmur is suspected but not positively identifiable, more advanced methods of detection can be used, such as an echocardiogram. If a murmur is detected during a routine veterinary exam, it is advisable to seek the opinion of a board-certified cardiologist.

With SAS there are often no symptoms at all prior to unexpected death. But a quick death is not always the case, and some dogs with severe SAS continue to live with increasing signs of heart failure. A dog with a mild murmur should live a normal life with mild exercise. The prognosis for more severe grades of SAS is grim. These cases are matters of maintenance and extreme moderation.

Because the presence of SAS is a matter of life and death, it is crucial that dogs with SAS murmurs never be bred.

SKIN DISORDERS

Among the most frustrating health problems for any dog owner are skin disorders. Unfortunately, Golden Retrievers have a reputation for skin problems, which usually appear due to an allergy or hot spots. While the actual allergy is not genetic, the predisposition for sensitivity is genetic, as is the tendency to have a poor immune system. On the other hand, some problems are helped along by the environment, neglect and improper management.

An extreme sensitivity to fleas is the cause of a majority of skin conditions. Besides scratching and chewing from the flea bites, which can irritate the skin, many dogs are allergic to flea saliva. Dogs have been known to chew and scratch themselves until they are raw. The skin becomes red and swollen and may even become infected. Once a problem has worked itself to this stage, radical treatment may be in order. This might include cortisone shots to stop the itching and swelling, and antibiotics for the infection. The long-time cure in any case is to rid the dog and its surroundings from fleas.

Reactions to other allergens can be equally severe. And it's not always easy to figure out what a dog is allergic to. Sometimes simply changing the diet may be enough, since food allergies are not uncommon. Other common allergies are to grass, especially when pollen is produced, and the chemicals used to produce carpeting.

As testing is not always conclusive and is difficult to interpret, some veterinarians begin by placing the patient on a special diet designed for dogs with skin problems and allergies, in an attempt to eliminate various possibilities. They may also prescribe pregnazone or cortisone to relieve the itching and scratching. This actually just avoids the problem, and may be creating new problems. Cortisone should never be used regularly over a long period of time unless it is absolutely needed, as it can significantly reduce the life span of a dog.

Skin problems can be created or made worse in an attempt to help the situation. Typical is the person who washes their dog to help the skin or get rid of fleas. Frequent baths and the use of harsh shampoos, or the failure to completely rinse the soap from the dog's skin and coat, can lead to dry skin, more scratching and irritation.

The addition or use of special diets may deprive the dog's body and skin of essential components and lead to increased problems as well. Unless an allergy to a specific food is known, it is best to keep to a well-balanced commercial dog food.

Obviously, there are no simple solutions to skin problems. They are a particular concern because they are not only uncomfortable for the dog but also affect us in almost every interaction with our dog. The dog may no longer look beautiful and might even smell. Figuring out the source of the problem and then adjusting the dog's diet or environment appears to be the best approach. Often the allergy is temporary and a dog will improve on its own, though credit for the improvement is given to the new diet or medication. Actual diagnosis and treatment of serious allergies is best done by a veterinary dermatologist.

Hot spots can be a real curse. They often seem to appear out of nowhere. They usually lie under a thick layer of coat and may be caused by a flea bite or some other irritation. A dog is especially prone to these during periods of shedding. The dog might chew at the spot, and if the area stays warm and moist, a bacterial infection flourishes. On the surface it is yellow and exudes puss.

Some Goldens seem to be susceptible to hot spots, possibly due to their coat and skin type, and seem to be constantly affected. Other Goldens may never get them, or only have one in a lifetime.

If the spots are caught in their earliest stages, they can often be controlled and eliminated by clipping the coat away from the sores and frequent washings with an antibacterial soap such as PhisoDerm. Diluted hydrogen peroxide and Sulfadene may also be helpful. Veterinary care may be needed for more serious and advanced cases.

Another skin problem is lick sores, which have no genetic basis but are included here because they are commonly encountered. These occur on the top of the front paws or the forelegs and ankles. They are most often seen in dogs that are inactive and bored. Some believe lick sores are an allergic response, rather than self-chewing to alleviate boredom. In any case, it becomes a bad habit. After constant licking, a red, shiny, hardened, hairless spot

forms. This itches and creates more chewing and licking. The area can become quite sore and even infected, requiring professional help.

Anti-lick sprays and cortisone are often used, but most dogs are so determined to lick themselves that any medication or preventive is licked off. Actual cortisone injection at the site can be useful, but rarely breaks the habit. A wide collar placed on the dog's neck, which prevents it from licking any part of its body, will allow the sore spot to heal. This barrier is only removed when the dog needs food and water. Some dogs are often so quick and devious that they will be back at partially healed spots in seconds if given the opportunity. If the barrier is left on for a long enough period of time, it can break the habit.

The expressive eyes of the Golden reflect the dog's emotional and physical feelings. (Dee Dee Anderson)

Another approach is to give the dog an occupation, keep it busy and provide enough exercise so that it is too tired to be bored.

HYPOTHYROIDISM

Hypothyroidism, where thyroid function falls below normal, is a common disorder that may affect Golden Retrievers. Hypothyroidism can be the root of many complex problems and is still poorly understood. The most common problem seen in a dog with low thyroid levels is extreme lethargy. Being overweight, poor skin and coat, irregular heat cycles and reproductive difficulties in both dogs and bitches are all attributed to low thyroid levels.

A blood test that separates and scores each of the various levels of the thyroid complex of hormones is a simple and relatively inexpensive way to diagnose the problem. A dog with hypothyroidism must take thyroxin daily for the rest of its life. The dosage may also have to be adjusted periodically. With this medication, most dogs lead normal lives.

If a dog shows signs of hypothyroidism but tests normal, it's important to look for another cause of its problems. The dog may just be very lazy, overfed for its activity level or have a skin allergy. Unfortunately, many problems can be interrelated and difficult to diagnose.

To add to the difficulty, many completely normal, active Golden Retrievers in good weight, coat and skin and with no reproductive problems show low thyroid levels when tested. Many veterinarians believe in routinely placing such a dog on thyroxin, despite their lack of symptoms. At this time, however, it is recommended that a Golden Retriever that shows no signs of low thyroid, yet tests low, should *not* be placed on an artificial thyroid replacement. It is suspected that as a whole, the Golden population has a different range of normal thyroid levels that it functions well on. Once a dog is placed on thyroxin, the body stops producing its own thyroid hormones and the dog must be kept on medication for the rest of its life. A normal dog should also never be placed on thyroid medication to increase coat or activity level in the hopes of making it more successful in the show ring.

The entire topic of hypothyroidism is controversial and one that requires much further research.

SEIZURES

One of the most frightening things for the dog owner to experience is a seizure in their dog. It is also probably one of the most mystifying and devastating problems affecting Golden Retrievers. Seizures vary in intensity and duration and have many causes. A mild seizure may be nothing more than a dog stiffening and then seeming to momentarily forget where it is, or lying on its side and paddling ineffectively for a brief period. This is called a *petite mal* seizure.

In a *grand mal* seizure, a dog paddles its legs furiously, foams at the mouth and defecates. The seizure may last for a minute or more. This dog will always be wobbly and extremely disoriented for a period of time afterwards. Owners of dogs that have frequent seizures learn to anticipate a seizure because a dog exhibits an aura, as if looking into space at unseen objects.

The causes vary and include poisons, illness, trauma to the skull, brain tumors and imbalances in the dog's chemistry. Idiopathic seizures—those that cannot be explained and occur frequently—are considered to be epilepsy. Epilepsy is thought to be genetic in origin if it appears before a dog is three years of age. Old age onset epilepsy, which occurs as early as five years, is equally common, and may also be genetic, or at least genetic in predisposition.

Nothing can be done to stop a seizure, and it is best to leave the dog alone, only making sure there is nothing around that it might hurt itself on. If poisoning is suspected or the seizure persists, the dog should receive emergency care.

A single seizure is not cause for immediate alarm. However, you should make an appointment with your veterinarian for a general exam and a blood chemistry profile to look for the cause. There is no need to place a dog on seizure preventive medication if the seizures are infrequent. If there is a pattern to the seizures and they appear to be occurring regularly, it is time to place a dog on daily doses of phenobarbital or another seizure-preventing drug. If the seizures still continue, the dosage should probably be increased. The medication itself is harmful to the dog's system and may shorten its life. However, dogs can die during a seizure, so when all the options are weighed, most vets recommend medication. It is most likely not the seizure itself that causes death, but the rupture of a blood vessel or heart failure due to the extreme stress a body is under during a seizure.

Many dogs lead fairly normal lives despite the regular occurrence of seizures. Others, once the pattern develops, decline quickly to the point where the seizures can no longer be controlled without the heaviest dosage of depressants.

A sound, healthy Golden is a reflection of a good genetic background and excellent care. (Janis Teichman)

Dogs that have seizures without any obvious reason and develop epileptic patterns should never be bred. If they have been bred, they should be immediately removed from any breeding program.

CANCER

This disease is mentioned only because its occurrence is seen so frequently in the breed. This is particularly true of lymphosarcoma, though other cancers are of equal concern. The particularly disturbing fact is that so many dogs in the prime of their lives are affected. Even more disturbing is that certain lines and families seem to have a higher incidence. There is no known way to prevent cancer, although there are many theories. All you can do is be aware of the danger signals and act quickly.

The lymph nodes, which are located throughout the dog's body, can be checked regularly for swelling. Cancer is only one of many problems that can cause the lymph nodes to

For a mild problem, attentive, loving care may be all that an adult dog needs. But puppies are more fragile and may need veterinary intervention. (Janis Teichman)

swell, but it is a useful sign. It is important to know what is normal for your dog. This is also true of its activity level and especially its food consumption. For many Goldens, the surest sign of illness is the lack of appetite, and this alone is cause for a veterinary visit.

Cysts, lumps on the skin and hard growths on the bones are visible forms of potential cancer problems and are simple for an owner to detect with routine grooming. Many cysts and lumps are benign and of no real danger to the dog. The existence of a malignant growth can only be confirmed by biopsy, although many veterinarians can tell by observation the difference between a sebaceous cyst and a malignant growth.

Some forms of cancer respond well to chemotherapy, and others move so quickly that no form of treatment is effective. When detected early and removed, the prognosis for a continued healthy life is good. The important thing is to know what is normal for the body.

WHEN TO CALL THE DOCTOR

Some situations need immediate care, and others require you to wait and see. Learning how to differentiate is something of an art, informed by experience. Vomiting and diarrhea are not, in themselves, reasons for emergency care in an adult dog, unless they are accompanied by a temperature over 101 degrees and the dog is listless. Many times these primary symptoms are caused by minor gastrointestinal disturbances that can be treated by removing food and giving Kaopectate. If the dog does not improve and the symptoms persist, veterinary care should be sought.

This is not the case when a puppy is involved. A puppy is more sensitive to illness, and the possibility of a weakness in the immune system, despite immunization, is a real threat. As soon as symptoms are recognized, a veterinarian should be contacted. Many times a puppy does not survive a virus simply because supportive care was delayed.

In the case of a dog that lacks appetite, it is a matter of knowing the eating habits of your own dog. If a dog never misses a meal but goes off its food for more than a day, look for veterinary advice. If a dog periodically leaves its food anyway, it is probably not a problem unless the dog is also depressed and listless.

Any time a dog has a fever it is time to call the doctor, as this is a sure sign of infection.

A first-time single seizure of short duration is reason for an appointment, but does not warrant an emergency call. If the seizure lasts for over a minute, or is followed right after by another, it is time for help.

Small cuts and wounds can often be treated at home, but if the entire first layer of epidermis is cut and the wound is nearly half an inch long, it will require a suture or two for proper healing. Puncture wounds should be thoroughly cleaned and flushed with hydrogen peroxide. An antibiotic shot may be in order to prevent infection.

Keeping a Golden healthy is a matter of prevention and common sense. A dose of good genetics certainly helps, but if things go wrong you should know what to do and have a veterinarian you trust to help you. That's why it is so important to establish a good relationship with a veterinarian *before* anything goes wrong.

(Lorraine Rodolph)

CHAPTER 7

Routine Care

The most anticipated event of the day for the average Golden Retriever is feeding time. The old saying that the way to the heart is through the stomach may be partially true for these dogs. It is certainly an important ingredient for a healthy, happy dog.

The normal Golden does best on a commercially produced dog food of premium quality. The market for quality dog foods has grown tremendously over the last two decades, and there are so many choices available that a decision may be difficult.

FEEDING A PUPPY

The choice may be simpler during puppyhood, as you may wish to continue with the food used by the breeder. This may not be possible though, because not all brands are available in all areas of the country. If you can't use the same brand, look for a puppy food that is highly palatable and easily digested. A commercially prepared dry food is the best choice for several reasons. It is the most reasonably priced in terms of cost per ounce. Canned foods are very expensive. They also do not provide the exercise to the teeth and gums that dry food provides. This form of oral exercise is especially important for a growing young mouth. Partially moist foods are preserved with sugars, an ingredient that is not needed in the dog's diet.

The main ingredients of any dog food are listed on the label. These should include some form of meat and some type of grain (corn, wheat, soy or rice). If the meat is listed as chicken or beef by-products, this means that the parts of an animal you would never consider to be edible have been used.

A good-quality food will use the better parts of the animal in its formula.

The percentages of protein, fat and fiber are also listed on the label, as well as the period of the dog's life for which the food is recommended. This is determined by regulated testing procedures.

Puppies need more protein and fat to meet the needs of their growing bodies. Protein percentages of 26 to 28 percent should be sufficient for stable growth. There are a number of foods designed for growth that list percentages as high as 38 percent. This much protein may be detrimental, because it encourages growth that is too rapid for good health. The fat percentages should be fairly high (about 17 percent) for proper absorption of nutrients and good skin and coat. The fiber content should be under 5 percent at this time of a dog's life, as fiber blocks the absorption of minerals and nutrients.

A puppy should initially be fed three to four times a day. It will usually let you know, by ignoring one of the feedings, when this can be cut back to fewer meals. You may want to add a small amount of water to the food, or it can be fed dry with water available.

A high-quality puppy food is so well balanced nutritionally that no supplements or other foods should be added. A daily vitamin tablet may be given, but nothing else should be needed. Adding meat or sauces to encourage a picky eater only makes the problem worse. If there really is a problem with digestibility, you will see other signs besides uneaten food. These may include excessive flatulence and loose stools.

As puppies get older, they can be fed less often during the day. (June Smith)

The recommended feeding amounts listed on the food bag may not be right for every puppy. Take the amount of food listed on the bag and divide it by the number of feedings per day to determine how much to give at each meal. So if the manufacturer recommends feeding one and a half cups of food a day, and you feed three times a day, then initially offer the puppy one half cup of food at each meal. If all of this is regularly devoured, it may be necessary to increase the amount of food. If the puppy is leaving food uneaten and is in good health and weight, cut back on the amount of food offered.

Some puppies and dogs are self limiting and eat only what they need. But gluttony is a common trait among Goldens, and many will eat as long as food is available. The best guideline is observation. If a puppy is in good weight and is growing steadily, then the amount is sufficient. If excess fat is accumulating, feed less. Fat puppies grow into fat dogs and are always prone to more structural and general health problems. Never let a puppy get fat.

A puppy should be fed in the same location all the time. This might be an area in the kitchen or the dog run. If it has been decided that a crate will be a part of the dog's environment, this can serve as an ideal place to enjoy a meal. Any uneaten food should be picked up and thrown away. Allowing a dog free access to food is not advisable, as it leads to food contamination. You are also unable to monitor how much the dog eats, which can be an important indicator of health.

A young dog should be fed twice daily and kept on puppy food through 12 months of age. During this time a dog will eat more food than it generally would as an adult, and the food is better digested and assimilated with two meals a day, rather than just one.

FEEDING AN ADULT DOG

The factors affecting the choice of an adult food are many. First of all, the food should be the best quality available at an affordable price. The food must be easily available and found in more than one location. It must provide all the nutrients a dog needs for its level of activity and lifestyle. Most important to the dog, it should taste good.

A good maintenance dog food will contain about 20 to 24 percent protein,

about 12 percent fat and just under 5 percent fiber. Diets high in protein and fat are only needed if a dog receives large amounts of exercise and training.

The adult dog is usually fed once a day, although many owners prefer to divide their dog's food into two meals. This is helpful for good digestion and may help to prevent bloat, a potentially fatal disorder. Bloat is caused by a build-up of gas in the stomach, causing it to become visibly swollen. The stomach may even twist on itself, a condition known as torsion. This situation is extremely painful and requires immediate veterinary attention. Some people pre-soak dry kibble in water before it is fed in an effort to prevent bloat.

The amount fed will depend on the composition of the food, the dog's activity level and how

Fresh water should always be available for drinking and standing in. (Linda Marchica)

The lean, well-muscled body of Red Rover's Risky Business, MH, WCX, is the result of regular training and exercise. (Janis Teichman)

its system functions. A medium-size adult Golden usually maintains good weight at three to four cups of dry food a day—but remember, different foods will require different amounts. As with a puppy, the best guideline for how much to feed is determined by the overall appearance of the dog. A good indication of proper weight is that the ribs can be felt, but are not apparent to the eye. A dog that gains unnecessary weight should have its intake reduced or be placed on a diet lower in fat and protein, with an increased percentage of fiber.

If you want to switch to another dog food, it should be done gradually, especially if the new food differs significantly in composition. During the first few days, feed 25 percent new food and 75 percent old food. After a few days, change to half old and half new. After a few more days, offer 75 percent new food and 25 percent old. Finally, feed just the new diet. The whole process should take about two weeks. The results of switching to a different food are almost never immediate, and it may take several months to notice any significant changes in your dog.

Supplements should be restricted to such items as a vitamin tablet, brewer's yeast or powdered kelp. There are many products available to enhance the skin and coat. But, hopefully, sound genetics and a good diet will provide everything a Golden needs.

EXERCISE

Puppies should be exercised carefully and in moderation. Good muscle development is important, but too much stress placed on a developing body can make mild structural problems severe. Short walks, shorter runs and short retrieves on flat ground, as opposed to rough terrain, are within the limits of a puppy. If littermates live nearby, or if there are puppy friends of similar size and age, play provides the best exercise possible.

Playing with other dogs is one of the best forms of exercise available. (Lorraine Rodolph)

Long walks and runs over a mile are well within the abilities of a full-grown Golden. For the sake of fitness and good health, a Golden should ideally receive some form of exercise every day. A missed day or two is of no real consequence.

How these needs are met varies, depending on available time and areas suitable for recreation. Some dogs are self-exercising—they run and pace in their yard all day. If there is more than one dog in the household, they often create their own exercise with chase and play games. The dog that lives by itself or does not voluntarily move unless it has a reason needs a human to get it started.

Retrieving is one of the best forms of exercise available. It does not require a large area. It need be only as far as you can throw a Frisbee, ball, bumper or stick. A 40-yard throw means the dog runs 80

Even when there is snow on the ground, 11-month-old Cali still gets out for a romp. (Stacy Brines)

When a dog is eight to 10 months old it has reached its basic adult size, though it may not actually be physically mature for several years. The amount of exercise can now be increased. Training periods can be longer and more physically demanding, though jumping and anything else that might jar growing bones should be avoided.

yards out and back. Ten of these is 800 yards, takes hardly any time and is nothing for a retriever. Twenty of these is almost a mile.

Swimming is another excellent form of exercise. Some dogs will swim alongside a person as they do laps in the family pool. Goldens have been known to do laps on their own.

If there is a pond or slow-moving stream nearby, these can also make great swimming spots. Always be sure that the water is free of toxins or anything else that might be harmful to a dog. Always comb areas used by fishermen for fish hooks and lines a dog might get tangled in, and fish carcasses with sharp bones.

A tennis ball and a swimming pool combine to make the perfect way for Molly to enjoy exercise on a warm day. (Sally Jenkins)

In the Pacific Northwest, the native salmon are host to a fluke that is poisonous to dogs, whether it is ingested raw or cooked. These fish, or parts of them, are often found on river banks and act as magnets for the parasites. In some parts of the country snakes and alligators are a real threat. And many lakes and streams are polluted. Make sure you understand your local water conditions before you let your dog in for a swim.

ROUTINE GROOMING

In relation to other breeds, Goldens have relatively few grooming needs. Their requirements are basic and easy for anyone to master. I'll look at how to take care of that lovely, golden coat in the next chapter. Here I'll deal with routine care of the ears, eyes, mouth, nails and anal glands. I will also include routine exams for lumps and bumps.

Normally, none of these areas need daily attention, unless you feel your dog's teeth need daily care or an ear problem exists.

ESSENTIAL EQUIPMENT

Curling up on the floor with a cat is the best thing to do after a hard day of work. (Jeanine Campbell)

There are tools, solutions and medications you will want to obtain for your grooming regimen. You will need a pair of nail clippers of either the guillotine or scissors type. If you are feeling extravagant, you may want to purchase a nail grinder and cauterizer, though the job can be done with less expensive tools.

The tools that might be needed to groom a Golden include mat splitters, combs, slicker brush, nail clippers, nail grinder, thinning shears and scissors. (J. Cairns)

Small scissors, cotton-tipped swabs, cotton balls, a toothbrush and tooth scalar should also be among your grooming tools. A commercially prepared ear cleansing solution, canine toothpaste, topical antibacterial eye ointment, Panalog, Kwik Stop, hydrogen peroxide, antibacterial soap, Kaopectate and an emergency supply of general antibiotics (which can sometimes be obtained from your veterinarian) should all be included in your supply box. These will be necessary for grooming and dealing with any minor health problems that might occur.

THE EARS

The inside of a healthy ear should look clean and emit no unpleasant odors. The inner ear of the Golden is well protected, as it is completely covered. This outward protection also acts to trap foreign objects and keeps moisture in the ear cavity, producing an ideal environment for infection. Because of this, the Golden's ear should be checked weekly, and cleaned if necessary. The outer extremes of the inner ear flap may have plain dirt, but it is in the ear canal itself that a waxy exudate accumulates.

The inner ear is cleaned by placing an ear cleansing solution into the ear. Massage the ears from the outside to loosen any dirt and accumulated wax. A dog will usually shake its head, and this will further loosen the dirt. Take a cotton ball or small cloth and wipe the outer ear and outside canal area clean. Cotton swabs can be used to get wax and dirt out of crevices in the outer ear canal.

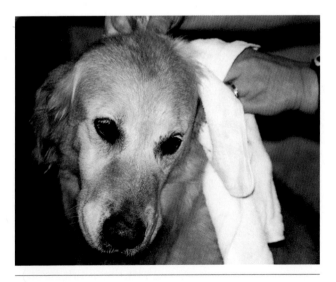

The outer ear is wiped clean with a small towel. (J. Cairns)

Never place any object deep into the ear. If wax build-up is excessive and a persistent foul odor is present, it is usually a sign of infection. This is when it is handy to have an antibiotic ointment, such as Panalog. This can be placed in the ear once or twice a day until a veterinarian can be consulted.

Ear infections are usually caused by an imbalance of wax production and the presence of bacteria. A foreign object in the ear is also a likely cause. If this is the case, a dog will usually hold its head to one side or shake the head frequently. Embedded foreign objects, such as grass awns, must be surgically removed.

Dogs that swim are likely candidates for ear problems that are created by water trapped in the ear canals. It is important to dry the ears thoroughly after a swim.

Shaking the head violently due to an ear problem can lead to hematoma. The shaking motion can cause a blood vessel in the ear to burst, and the ear flap then becomes engorged with blood. The ear will actually look like a small pillow, which is how the common term for this condition, "pillow ear," is derived. If left untreated, the hematoma eventually shrinks and dries up, but the ear is left misshapen. The ear should be surgically drained for proper healing.

THE EYES

There is actually no maintenance required of the eyes, other than checking them weekly for any foreign objects that might be under the lids or in the corner of the eye. Generally, a disturbance to the eye is so noticeable that it is immediately recognized. The ophthalmic ointment in your grooming kit should be available in case a slight injury or eye infection is suspected. This is for use only until you can get to a veterinarian.

Some Goldens have extremely long eyebrows, and those with curly coats often have eyebrows that turn in towards the eye itself. If your Golden fits this description, keep the eyebrows trimmed to prevent irritation.

THE MOUTH AND TEETH

Most people ignore the importance of canine dental care. The teeth of a young dog are clean and well formed, and it is easy to forget that the teeth change as a dog ages. Just like people, some dogs seem to have naturally sound teeth, while others need constant dental attention.

The build-up of tarter, which leads to gum disease and tooth loss, can only be prevented by regular cleanings. Dogs that are avid chewers of Nylabones or knuckle bones tend to have cleaner teeth from the chewing action, but this is not always enough to prevent problems. Even if you feel routine brushing and scaling is not necessary, the dog should be accustomed to having its mouth and teeth examined, in case problems do crop up.

Basic cleaning consists of no more than brushing the teeth with a toothbrush and canine toothpaste (never use toothpaste for humans!). A small towel wrapped around your index finger can also be used instead of the brush.

Tarter builds up primarily on the back molars of both jaws, and first appears close to the gum

Every Golden puppy should become accustomed to having its mouth and teeth examined. (Janis Teichman)

THE NAILS

Proper care of the nails is a simple part of basic grooming, but one that many owners and their dogs find unpleasant. A dog should become used to having its nails trimmed as a puppy. Even if the nails do not need cutting, go through the motions anyway, and at least a sliver of nail should be removed once a week. If you make this a pleasant, routine chore for the puppy, the adult will tolerate it quite well.

Goldens differ in their nail care requirements. Those that exercise on surfaces that cause natural wear, such as concrete, may seldom need attention. The bone structure and placement of the foot also affects nail growth. Dogs with correct front assemblies and good foot structure seldom need the nail care that a less well-put-together dog requires.

line. If caught in its early stages, it can be easily scrapped off with a tooth scaler, or even your fingernail. This becomes more difficult as the amount of tarter increases, and attempts at removal can lead to cut gums. At this point, a professional cleaning by a veterinarian is probably in order.

In cases of severe gum disease, the tooth is so enveloped by tarter that it is barely visible. This causes the tooth and its root system to rot, which is obvious by the presence of offensive odors. A dog may have difficulty eating, and the area of the face or jaw near the infected tooth becomes swollen. Regular dental care will keep the mouth healthy and prevent tooth-related problems from occurring.

The toenails of the Golden are light in color, though a dark strip of pigment may run down the top of the nail. This makes the decision of where to clip easier. The slight hook that forms after leaving the base of the nail is where you should cut. A small vein runs down the middle of each nail. This is called the quick, and if cut, it will bleed. If this occurs, apply a styptic powder, such as Kwik Stop, to the bleeding tip. Pressure on the cut end can also be applied to stop the bleeding. Inexpensive cauterizers specifically sold for bleeding nails are extremely effective. Try not to cut the quick, as this will likely make nail cutting an unpleasant experience for your dog.

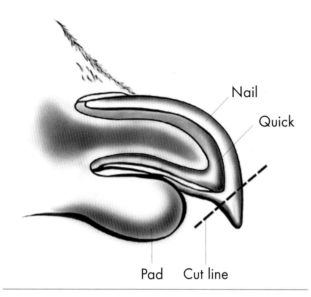

Nail

Quick

Pad   Cut line

The Golden nail is light colored and should be clipped where the hook forms. Take care so the quick is not accidentally cut.

If you cannot master the use of standard nail clippers, consider buying an electric nail grinder. These are basically electric filing wheels that grind down the nail. They are more expensive and are noisy, but they work quickly and reduce the chances of cutting the nail too short. They produce a nice, smooth, rounded nail.

The nails of both the front and rear feet should be clipped or checked every two weeks. The surest sign that nails need to be clipped is the sound of clicking nails as they hit a hard floor. In the home, long nails can scratch floors and damage carpeting and anything else they might encounter.

Nails left untrimmed can be responsible for deforming the foot. As the nails become long, the toes spread out to support the weight of the dog's body. This causes the feet to splay and they are reduced in their function, creating a dog that for all purposes is crippled. Very long nails can also curl under the foot pads, creating pain every time the dog takes a step.

THE ANAL GLANDS

Care of the anal glands is the most unpleasant part of routine canine care. Sacks are located around the anus that accumulate secretions. When they are full, a dog becomes uncomfortable and will attempt to relieve the situation by scooting along the floor or ground in a sitting position. This may work fine, but the place the dog chooses may be the living room carpet.

Removing these secretions is called expressing the glands. When pressure is applied to the edge of the sides of the anus, the contents of the sacks are released. If you decide to do this yourself, be sure to hold a paper towel or cloth between your hand and the dog. This is a foul smelling liquid, and it can be expressed with some force.

The best time to express the glands is just before a dog is bathed, as anything that gets on the dog can be washed off. If a dog is professionally groomed, this is something that can be requested along with the bath.

Sometimes the glands become plugged up or impacted. This is always painful and may lead to infection. At this point, veterinary attention is needed.

THE TACTILE EXAM

After all your routine grooming chores are done, you need to go over your dog with your hands. Start at the head and neck, and work down the shoulders to the front legs. Then feel the back, sides and stomach. Finally, examine the rear end, legs and tail. You are asking your hands to feel for any lumps or bumps, anything abnormal that might be on the body that your eyes cannot detect.

If you do this exam regularly, you should always be up to date and aware of anything that might be different or require attention. You and your dog will also enjoy the physical closeness of a tactile exam.

THE PROFESSIONAL GROOMER

If you feel you are just not able to do these routine tasks, you need to schedule regular appointments with a professional groomer. The professional dog groomer can be one of a dog's best friends and spot problems long before they become apparent to the owner or even a veterinarian.

Selecting a groomer is similar to finding a veterinarian. Ask for recommendations from other people with dogs, dog clubs or even your veterinarian. Some veterinary clinics offer grooming services, so the solution may be simple.

The groomer must be someone who exudes confidence and inspires trust. Their shop should be

An exuberant attitude and love of life is only possible with a good diet, exercise and regular grooming. (American Kennel Club)

clean and businesslike. Their holding areas for animals before and after they are groomed should be secure and free of foul odors. The normal services offered with a bath include brushing, nail clipping, ear cleaning, expressing the anal glands and trimming the feet of excess hair. Extra brushing due to matting and shedding may cost more.

Since most Goldens do not require a bath as often as they need their ears cleaned and nails clipped, more frequent appointments for just these services may be scheduled at a reduced price. Some groomers even offer these services on a walk-in basis.

(Mary Bloom)

CHAPTER 8

The Golden Coat

The Golden Retriever coat varies so much from dog to dog that no single set of grooming procedures can be used on all members of the breed. Coats range from short to long, thin to thick and straight to curly. What is suitable for the coat of one Golden Retriever may be totally inadequate or excessive for another.

How frequently a dog is brushed and bathed will depend upon the owners' personal preferences and what is needed to keep the coat attractive and healthy.

BRUSHING

Brushing keeps the coat free of foreign objects, promotes the health of the hair and skin, removes loose, dead hair and stimulates new hair growth. Regardless of coat type, all Goldens should, at a minimum, be brushed weekly. This is fine for the correct, nearly maintenance-free coat described in the breed standard, but will not work for a heavily coated dog. Brushing can be a part of your weekly overall grooming and examination sessions.

A slicker brush works well on the average Golden coat. This brush has long wire pins that are bent at the ends. Begin at the front of the dog and work back, being sure to thoroughly brush the neck and throat and underneath the ears.

The feathers of the legs and tail are a catchall for burrs and debris. A comb may work better on the feathering, depending on the coat. The back and side of the dog are the easiest to brush and are most enjoyable for the dog.

Mats of hair form into tight clumps when a dog scratches or chews a particular area excessively, or when an area is not properly groomed. Mats are most likely to be found underneath the ears and in the feathering of the legs and tail. If they have just started to form, they can sometimes be brushed or combed out or removed with a mat splitter. Mats on the legs and tail can usually be safely cut out with scissors.

As mats become larger, they work their way closer to the skin, becoming painful for the dog. This makes their removal by scissors risky, especially when they are under the ears. It is easy to cut skin

A slicker brush works well on the coat. Brush the dog from front to back. (Mary Bloom)

A comb may be better for the feathering on the legs and tail. (Mary Bloom)

rather than hair when they occur in this area. This is when the services of a professional groomer are called for. These mats can be removed quickly and safely with electric clippers. Another location mats occur that may need expert removal is between the toes or between the pads of the feet. Mats form in these areas when dogs chew on their feet.

During periods of heavier shedding, you will want to brush your dog more frequently. At this time the old undercoat dies and becomes loose. It needs to be removed for the best growth of a nice new undercoat. An excellent way to help loosen this hair is to rub your hands through the coat, massaging the skin of the shoulders, neck, back, sides and rear legs. This can also be done during seasons when shedding is very light. The dead coat comes out much more quickly with this kind of help. A grooming rake works particularly well to remove dead undercoat, taking it out in huge chunks.

Long hair and thick coats are more difficult to maintain. A heavily coated Golden will need more

During periods of heavy shedding, a dog will need more brushing. This owner is using a pin brush for the longer hair on the chest. (Mary Bloom)

frequent brushing. Ignoring such a coat for even a week can lead to a major overhaul job. Goldens that have been neutered or are on thyroid medication usually grow excessive undercoat. This appears as a soft, downy fur that grows out through the outer coat. This soft hair is more likely to mat and also requires additional brushing. The Golden with a curly coat often needs special attention, especially if that coat is long, dense and curly. It is more likely to collect foreign objects and mat. The short curly coat is relatively trouble free.

BATHING

How often you bathe your dog is generally a personal choice, rather than one of necessity. It is usually recommended that a Golden never be bathed more than once every six to eight weeks. This is a guideline based on the needs of a working retriever's coat. The coat and skin need a balance of natural oils for proper protection from the elements. A dog that is frequently in the water needs these oils to keep it as dry and warm as possible. A correctly coated retriever shakes after getting out of the water and is nearly dry. This is true for Goldens, as well as the other retriever breeds. Excessive bathing is believed to destroy the natural balance of these oils.

It may be surprising to hear that many Goldens never receive more than a handful of baths in their entire lives! These are not cases of neglect. These dogs receive frequent brushings and proper care, are parasite free, live primarily in the house and usually swim regularly, and that is enough.

However, not all Goldens have the type of coat that can be managed like this, nor can their owners tolerate the odors that may be associated with a dog. The odor of most coats is only readily apparent when the dog is outdoors most of the time, kept in a run that is not clean or just before shedding, when the undercoat tends to hold in moisture and build up smells.

Goldens can be bathed more frequently than the recommended six to eight weeks. Show dogs are bathed before every weekend they are out, and many are bathed just before they go into the ring every time they are shown, which could be every day.

Regardless of how often you choose to bathe your dog, the shampoo you use must be of the best quality possible. Suitable shampoos, ones that clean as well as supplement and replenish the coat with essentials the shampoo may have removed, can usually be purchased from pet supply stores, groomers or veterinarians. If you're not sure what to buy, call a dog groomer and ask for their recommendation for the breed.

Many shampoos that are commercially available are too harsh for a dog's skin and coat and should never be used. But the best shampoo in the world will

Too much bathing will remove the oils a Golden needs to keep it warm and comfortable in the water. (Janis Teichman)

still harm a dog's skin if the dog is not rinsed completely. Soap that is left in the coat will cause irritation, rash and skin problems.

Baths can be given indoors or outdoors, but use common sense. If it is a nice warm day, there is no reason why a bath outside with water from the hose will not work. It is another matter though if the weather is cool. An indoor bath tub is the next location of choice, and here you have the luxury of heated water. Puppies and older dogs should be bathed indoors with warm water to prevent chill. Hose attachments can be purchased to fit to the faucet, which makes bathing much easier.

Unless a dog is covered with mud or has been sprayed by a skunk, be sure it is well brushed before the bath. If there are mats in the coat, bathing will set them in even tighter and make their removal more difficult. In addition, the penetration of water and shampoo will be more effective if as much loose hair as possible has been removed.

Start by wetting the dog thoroughly from head to tail. Be sure to get the underside, legs and throat wet. The water may seem to literally roll off the dog, leaving it dry. If this happens, work your hand through the coat as the water hits the body for better absorption.

Begin rinsing at the head and work down, using your hands to squeeze the soap and water out of the coat. The areas that are most likely to retain soap are the ruff of the neck and the underside, where it is difficult to get water. The rinsing is complete when no more soap suds come out of the coat with pressure from your hand. A good rule to follow is to rinse until the soap is gone and then rinse for another minute more.

DRYING THE COAT

Remove any excess water from the coat by squeezing the hair, and then rub the dog down with a towel until it is as dry as possible.

Be sure there is no water in the ears. If it is a nice warm day, a healthy dog can self-dry. If the weather is cool and a warm place to dry off is not available, it is best to use a dryer. A regular hand-held hair dryer can be used on a moderate setting. Brush the coat while using the dryer, and the dog will come out looking lush and fluffy. Commercial dog dryers that fit on a crate and blow warm air into the crate area, or large standing blow dryers are essential equipment if you have several dogs and plan to show them.

TRIMMING

The Golden coat is meant to be natural and free of the clipping and scissoring required of other breeds. But sometimes a little trimming is required. The most obvious place trimming is needed is the feet. Shaping the hair to the contour of the feet is

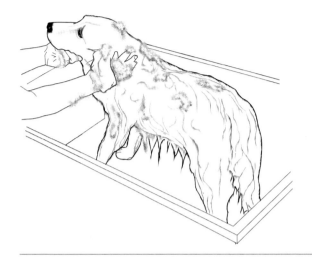

The soap is applied on the back and the lather is worked throughout the dog's body. Take care to avoid getting soap near the dog's eyes.

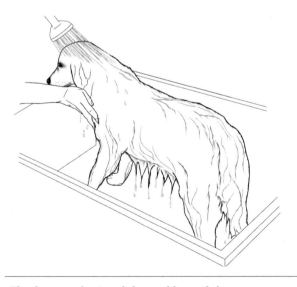

The dog must be rinsed thoroughly until there are no more soap suds.

not only neater in appearance, it also prevents excess dirt from being brought into the house. A pair of scissors should be all that is needed.

The hair on the bottom of the foot is cut so that it is even with the pads. The dog will then walk solely on its pads, rather than on a layer of hair. Trim the hair around the outside of the foot so that a clean outline of the foot is presented. Excess hair grows between the toes. This can be combed upwards and then trimmed so that it is even with the toes on the top of the foot.

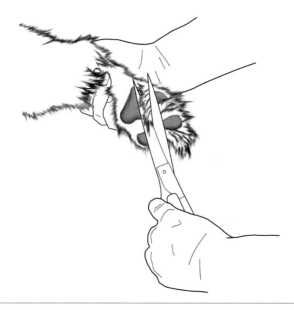

The hair on the bottom of the foot is trimmed so that it is flush with the pads.

The hair on the back of the hocks and pasterns can be evened up if it tends to be long. For the sake of cleanliness and maintenance, you may wish

A clean, well-groomed Golden. (American Kennel Club)

to trim the hair around the tail and anus. Hunters often shorten the feathers and ruffs of their Goldens to prevent them from picking up burrs. This type of grooming is a matter of preference and the individual coat of the dog.

As I've already mentioned, Goldens that have been neutered often develop excessive undercoat that grows through the outer coat. This usually appears around the shoulders and the sides of the thighs. This hair has a tendency to pick up foreign objects and mats more easily than the normal coat. The coat will appear more attractive if this soft fur is scissored so that it is even with the outer coat. It also usually pulls out easily. This might work if it appears in thin sporadic patches, but not if it is extensive.

Frequent brushing, occasional trimming and a bath when needed with a quality shampoo should keep the Golden coat attractive and trouble-free. Common sense and the individual requirements of each dog are your best guides to proper coat care.

(Susie Rezy)

CHAPTER 9

Showing the Golden Retriever

A ny Golden Retriever owner will tell you that their dog is the most beautiful Golden in the world. The attempt to prove this point is probably how dog shows first developed. In this country, dog shows were once social events for wealthy dog owners and true sportsmen who gathered to determine how their stock measured up to other specimens of the same breed.

Dog shows have changed in many ways over the years, but in some ways they have not changed at all. At one time most shows were benched—the dogs were actually attached by chain to wooden benches and were available for viewing during the hours of the dog show, except when they were in the ring or had been excused. This is where the terms bench show, or bench champion, originated.

Only five shows are still benched in the United States (the dogs are kept on leashes or in crates now), including Westminster, but dog shows are still fun to attend, and you can still meet plenty of dogs.

The world of showing dogs is fun, exciting and full of frustrations. It is a wonderful way to meet other fanciers and make friendships that last a lifetime. You never cease to learn new things at dog shows, where new research, canine products and technologies are introduced and discussed. Whether your goal is success in the classes or the ultimate success of completing a Championship, you will have gained knowledge and enjoyment by participating in an activity with your dog.

All-breed shows are open to registered dogs of all recognized breeds. A specialty show is for one specific breed. It may be held as a separate show, or in conjunction with an all-breed show. There are also a few group shows, where all the breeds in a particular AKC-designated group, such as the Sporting Group (of which the Golden is a member), are exhibited.

Many shows are held as part of a cluster. A cluster may be two or more shows held at the same location on successive days, or the shows may be located very close to each other. These shows in close proximity are sometimes called a circuit, especially if there are several shows in the same general area over a period of a couple of weeks. Exhibitors like clusters and circuits because in one trip they can have several chances to win points towards their dog's Championship.

The purpose of a dog show is to evaluate how a

This dog is ready for the ring. Note the well-groomed feet, trimmed whiskers and show lead. (American Kennel Club)

A judge examines the rear assembly of a dog. (Lorraine Rodolph)

dog measures up to its respective breed standard, and by comparison, how it ranks with other members of its breed present on that day. These dogs are then awarded placements first through fourth. A dog is judged solely on its conformation to the standard, its overall appearance and how it moves when gaited. Gaiting is important because proper structure and movement are interrelated.

A dog's intelligence, trainability and skills are not under consideration, although obvious temperament flaws cannot be ignored.

REQUIREMENTS FOR AN AKC CHAMPIONSHIP

The title Champion indicates that a dog is free of disqualifying faults as designated by the breed standard and is a good representative of the breed, in the opinion of at least three judges. To become a Champion, a dog must earn a total of 15 points. These points are awarded based on the number of dogs in the ring that day—the more dogs, the more points. However, the number of dogs required for points varies with the breed, sex and geographical location of the show. The AKC makes up a schedule of points each year to help equalize competition from breed to breed and area to area.

Dogs can earn from one to five points at a show. A win of three, four or five points is called a *major.* The 15 points required for a Championship must be won under at least three different judges, and must include two majors won under different judges.

At every show there are five class divisions: Puppy, Novice, American-Bred, Bred-by-Exhibitor and Open. Dogs and bitches are judged separately at this level. After the class judging is completed, the winners of each class re-enter the ring and the judge selects the best of each sex, called Winners Dog and Winners Bitch. These are the only two dogs in the breed awarded points towards their championship.

BEYOND THE CLASSES

Best of Breed competition comes after the classes. At this time, dogs that are already champions enter the ring, along with the Winners Dog and Winners Bitch. The selections this time are for Best of Breed (BOB). The dog so honored will go on to the Group judging. A Best of Opposite Sex (BOS) is also selected—opposite to whatever sex dog won Best of Breed.

Then, between the Winners Dog (WD) and Winners Bitch (WB), a Best of Winners (BW) is selected. This can be an important award, because sometimes more points are available for one sex in a breed than another. But whichever dog wins Best of Winners gets the most points available. So, for example, if more points are available for dogs than for bitches at a particular show, and the bitch is deemed Best of Winners, she will get the number of points that were available for the dogs.

Once a dog has completed its Championship, its show career can be continued by entering the Best of Breed class. These dogs are called *specials,* and can be entered in shows sporadically or campaigned very seriously. If a dog loves the ring and has the personality and eye-catching qualities necessary to be noticed in Group competition, a

Many people stay after breed judging to watch the Group competition and cheer on their breed. (American Kennel Club)

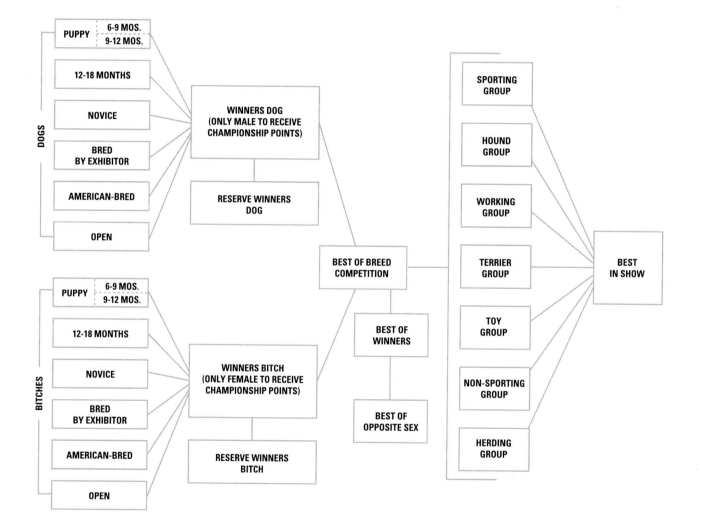

serious career may be considered. Membership in the Golden Retriever Club of America Show Dog Hall of Fame is earned by accumulating points from Group placements and Best in Show wins.

Don't let anyone tell you that the winners in a dog show are all a forgone conclusion. Anything can and does happen. A bitch can come from a Puppy class and go on to be WB, BW, BOB and on to the Group!

Winning a Best in Show is a lifelong dream for many fanciers. All dogs entered in a dog show on any day are eligible for this honor. The selection is a process of weeding out that begins at the class level and culminates in the selection of each BOB.

The Sporting Group winner is selected from among all the Best of Breed representatives in that group. This includes all retrievers, pointers, setters and spaniels. The seven Group winners go on to compete against each other, and it is from among these that Best in Show is awarded.

It may be difficult at first to understand how dogs of different breeds can be judged together. Just remember that they are not judged against each other. Rather, each dog is judged according to its individual breed standard. The dog that, in the judge's opinion, comes the closest to embodying its standard is the winner.

STARTING A SHOW CAREER

Before embarking on a show career, it may be wise to ask the advice and opinion of others who know your breed and can give you an honest appraisal of

Evaluating a puppy as a future show prospect is difficult. Early training serves to teach a puppy to stand properly. This is Golden Pines Maui Waltz at nine weeks old. (Janis Teichman)

the quality of your dog. Trying to evaluate a dog by reading the breed standard may lead to incorrect interpretations if you are a novice. Some features and obvious faults are easy to spot, but others, such as angulation, are only really understood by a knowledgeable eye and experience. Obtaining an unbiased opinion may be difficult, and sometimes it is advisable to seek advice from someone who has experience showing another breed for an honest appraisal.

If you bought your puppy as a show prospect, you may be obliged to show it, unless circumstances prevent you from doing so. As the puppy matures, it is time to contact the breeder and begin with their appraisal.

HANDLING CLASSES

Even though it is the dog that is being judged, the handler at the end of the lead is just as important. There are handling skills that will help in the overall presentation of the dog that may make the difference between winning points and never even being considered. Handling classes are designed to teach the prospective handler the dos and don'ts of the breed ring and how to present a dog to its best advantage.

Classes may be offered by professional trainers or dog clubs. At these classes one is taught how to stack a dog in order to present the best view of the dog's conformation. The dog is taught to bait, which means the dog is alert and at attention on command, with the aid of food or a toy. The handler is taught how to move their dog individually, how to execute patterns in the ring and how to move their dog as the group moves for preliminary and final evaluation.

Handling classes are useful also for experienced handlers as a way to accustom young dogs to other dogs, handlers and ring experience.

It will also be necessary to learn what type of grooming is required for the show Golden. The breed should be presented as naturally as possible, so much less preparation is required than with many other breeds. Still, the Golden will need to be bathed and blown dry. The nails should be short

Practice your handling skills before you get into the ring, so you and your dog will be ready to look your best. (Janis Teichman)

and the hair on the feet trimmed to show the contour of the foot. Hair on the hocks and pasterns can be neatened and the whiskers can be trimmed, although this is not required or recommended for a working dog. Stray hairs on the ears, neck and tail can be trimmed for a neater appearance. Additional grooming secrets can be learned from experience and from other handlers.

MATCH SHOWS

One way to gain ring experience is to attend match shows. These may be AKC sanctioned, where clubs and judges gain credit and necessary experience for AKC approval, or just fun matches. They are conducted in exactly the same way as licensed shows, but are designed for experience only, with no points awarded. This is an excellent way to get your dog and yourself accustomed to the show environment and get over the pre-ring jitters.

A match show is the place to discover that there is more equipment you need before you jump into the real world of dog shows. If you've been to a handling class you already have a nice show lead, but there is probably more equipment you've never considered. These items might include special brushes and combs, fine scissors to trim a stray hair and an exercise pen or crate to contain the dog when it is not in the ring.

This well-groomed dog is waiting for its turn in the ring at the Westminster Kennel Club show. (American Kennel Club)

A cart with wheels to transport the crate or pen from the car to the show site is also very handy. A cover for the crate may be necessary, and a spray bottle for water and even a folding chair for the handler are also good items to have with you at shows.

FINDING THE DOG SHOWS

There are regional publications that print the dates and locations of licensed dog shows. The *AKC Gazette* publishes a supplement called *Events Calendar* that lists dog shows well in advance of the date. You can call the AKC at (919) 233-9767 to subscribe.

All dog shows are put on by dog clubs, but the majority are under the direction of a superintendent.

There are a number of these throughout the country, and you can ask them to put you on their mailing list. The *Events Calendar* contains a list of all licensed show superintendents. When you're at a show, the superintendent will also have information about other upcoming shows. The superintendent is also the person to ask for information about an upcoming show or an entry form.

When you've decided you're ready to take the big step and have called the superintendent for an entry form, you need to decide which class to enter. Some novice handlers mistakenly enter all the classes for which their dog may be eligible. However, the best advice is to stick with one class. Any dog over the age of six months is eligible for the Open class. But this is usually where the most mature dogs and

Last-minute grooming takes place up on the table. (American Kennel Club)

competitive handlers show. If your dog is a puppy, the best place for it is the 6-to-9-, 9-to-12- or 12-to-18-Month Puppy class. As the name implies, the Novice class is an excellent place for a beginner. After three wins in this class, a dog must move on to one of the other three levels. Bred-by-Exhibitor is for dogs handled by their breeder. It serves as a showcase for the proud breeder-handler. The American-Bred class was first developed to encourage Americans to breed their own champions, rather than import them from other countries. Now it is a good intermediate spot for the dog and handler out of Novice, but not quite ready for Open.

When reading the premium list the superintendent will send (a schedule for the show, including who will be judging), always be sure to note

This Golden is stacked for the judge's review. (Susie Rezy)

The judge examines the rear of the dog while the handler holds the head. (Kathy Wood)

the closing date. That is the date by which all entries and payments must be received. Dogs shows are very strict about this date and do not make exceptions. You will receive a confirmation that your entry was received, along with the ring number, the time your breed will be judged and your dog's entry number. This is when the adrenaline begins to flow and the jitters appear.

YOUR FIRST SHOW

Good or bad, your first show is always etched in your memory permanently. This is the beginning of a great adventure. You will learn how to travel and find motels that take dogs. You will learn how to bathe your dog on the road and discover everything you forgot to bring. You will learn about how to find show sites, find a parking place and how to lug everything to the ring in one trip.

Your entry confirmation lists the scheduled starting time for your breed. You should be at the ring, ready to check in, at least 15 minutes before the time listed. Every ring has a steward's table located near the ring entrance. Stewards are hard-working volunteers who assist the judge. A steward is in charge of checking in dogs and handlers and distributing numbered arm bands. They make sure handlers and dogs of the correct class are ready to enter the ring at the proper time. Upon arriving at ringside, let the steward know your class and number. You will be given an arm band that must be placed on the upper left arm. If you fail to check in, you will be marked absent and will be unable to compete when the class enters the ring.

As the time for judgment draws near, be ready near the ring with your dog. The steward will line you up with other handlers to enter the ring in some semblance of catalogue order. When all handlers and dogs are in the ring, the judge will instruct all competitors to circle the ring. This serves as a preview and helps to loosen everyone up. After stopping, it is time to stack your dog for individual examinations. Watch the judge, and have your dog in its best stance as he or she gets closer.

After looking over all the dogs at a trot and standing still, the judge will examine each one

The handler moves the dog in a pattern so the judge can observe its gait. (American Kennel Club)

individually. Usually each handler will bring their dog to the front of the ring for the individual examination. The judge will first approach the dog, then examine its structure for angulation, substance and coat texture.

The head, eyes and ear placement are all noted. The judge will ask you to open the dog's mouth so that the teeth and bite can be examined. On male dogs, the judge will check that both testicles are fully descended. Then the judge will ask you to move your dog in a pattern, so that gait may be observed. Watch other handlers that have preceded you and listen closely to the judge's instructions.

The pattern may be as simple as straight down and back, or a more involved triangular pattern,

The handler keeps his dog alert and looking its best even when not under direct examination. (American Kennel Club)

Upon returning, the judge will want to see alertness and expression—which makes this a good time to bait the dog.

Even after the judge has gone over your dog, keep it looking at its best just in case they decide to take a quick look back for comparison.

After all the dogs have been examined, the judge will request that all dogs once again be moved around the ring as a group. If the class is relatively small, placements will be given out at this time. A quick point of the finger will indicate first through fourth place. The dogs that did not place are excused. The placing dogs should remain in the ring, at the spots designated for the winners, so

The Best of Opposite Sex winner Golden Pine's Maui Waltz, CD is photographed in show stack with handler Nancy Kelly. (Janis Teichman)

where dog and handler positions should be changed for the best view. Try to keep your dog in an easy trot, where movement can be best observed.

that the judge and steward have a chance to record the proper arm band numbers in the results book. If a class is extremely large, it may be split or the judge may move dogs up or down in line as he or she makes decisions.

If you have been the lucky winner of a class, you must remain near the ring for the Winners class.

At the conclusion of the Open class for each sex, the winners of the previous classes are invited back to the ring for the Winners class. A similar judging procedure follows. This time the awards are Winners Dog, Winners Bitch and the Reserve Winner in each sex. If for some chance the Winners Dog is found to be ineligible, the points will be transferred to the Reserve Winner.

SHOW ETIQUETTE

Proper etiquette and sportsmanlike behavior is a must for anyone looking for long-term success in any dog-related sport. As this specifically applies to dog shows, it encompasses everything from appearance to your every action. You are not only responsible for yourself, but also for the behavior of your dog.

Good sportsmanship and politeness begins with checking in at ringside on time and being ready to enter the ring when called. At all times speak respectfully to the stewards and the judge. Be polite and gracious to fellow exhibitors. Always congratulate the winner and be as accepting of defeat as of success.

Your behavior as a dog owner is equally important. A dog must never be a nuisance to other dogs or people. When not on the other end of a lead, it should be safely confined. Excessive barking and aggression of any kind is not tolerated under any situation. A dog must never be abused or visibly corrected. Anytime a dog relieves itself it should be cleaned up and disposed of properly.

This code of proper dog management applies not only to the show grounds, but also to any lodging accommodations. Over the years it has become increasingly difficult to find motels that accept dogs due to the thoughtlessness of careless dog owners.

Good grooming and cleanliness of the dog is of primary concern to a handler, but the handler's appearance is of equal importance. While you need not dress for a formal occasion, a suit and tie is proper ring attire for a man and a comfortable skirt or nice pants suit is proper for a woman.

Unsportsmanlike behavior does not go unreported or ignored. Serious fines and suspensions are the punishment for anyone found guilty of any kind of verbal or physical abuse to animal or human at an AKC-licensed event. Dogs that exhibit unprovoked aggressive behavior towards other dogs or humans are excused for that day. They can be barred for life from participation of any kind if reported and written up by a judge on three occasions.

THE PROFESSIONAL HANDLER

Despite the pleasure and joy that can be derived from showing your own dog, at some point you

Proper attire and good grooming in the ring is as important for you as it is for your dog.
(American Kennel Club)

may decide you need the help of a professional handler. It may be because time constraints prevent you from attending shows, or you may have decided that a professional could do a better job of presenting your dog in the ring. Winning is what professionals are best at—this is why they are paid. They have a knack for showing a dog at its best and getting a judge's attention.

The selection of a handler should be made carefully. As always, ask for advice from others you trust. Observe various professionals at work. Are they neat? Are they polite? Do their dogs appear happy and in the best possible condition? In other words, do they conduct themselves in a professional manner?

Talk to each prospective handler and set up an appointment. Discuss how your dog will be cared for and kenneled when it is with the handler. Depending on the circumstances, they may or may not want to exhibit your dog. Some may be honest enough to decline because of the lack of quality of the dog. Many popular professionals have waiting lists and their services are unavailable.

Letting a professional take over is a difficult decision. Entrusting the care of your "baby" for the sake of a title is not the right choice for everyone.

(Laurie Berman)

CHAPTER 10

The Golden Retriever in the Field

The retriever breeds were originally developed as non-slip hunting dogs. This meant that they did not find game (this was the job of the setter, pointer or spaniel), but once the bird was located, flushed and shot, the retriever's job was to find the bird and return it to the hunter. The other hunting breeds were not expected to retrieve. Retrievers were discovered to be especially useful in waterfowl hunting due to the nature of their build, coat, marking and swimming abilities.

One man tells the story of how when he was a young boy, his father would take him along hunting to a nearby lake. It was usually cold, often with snow on the ground and ice on the water. When his father shot a duck that landed in the lake, he would tie a rope around his son and tell him to go out and get the bird. The rope was to help him get out if the ice broke. After returning with the bird, the boy was sent to the cab of the truck to warm up and wait for the next retrieve. This is a true story and a modern one at that, and it points out what a hunter will use to retrieve birds if a dog is not around—and probably what was used before retrievers were developed.

In the real world of hunting, Goldens are used to produce and retrieve game. Due to their outstanding scenting abilities, they are excellent at quartering upland game. Some point and hold naturally and can be taught to flush a bird on command. They are useful for dove, quail, pheasant, chukar, grouse or any other upland bird that might be hunted regionally. Unlike the pointers and setters, they work closer to the hunter and at a reasonable pace.

Goldens are regarded as having the best nose of the retriever breeds, and so are the most satisfactory for upland game. Many people prefer the Chesapeake Bay and Labrador Retrievers for waterfowl, because of their coats, but a Golden is perfectly adequate for retrieving geese and ducks in almost all conditions.

A handler brings a dog to the line for a water blind at a hunting test. (Janis Teichman)

WHAT A GOOD RETRIEVER NEEDS

A good retriever that is a pleasure to hunt with displays certain traits, some of which are innate and others of which are acquired through training. The natural abilities include marking, scenting, birdiness, the desire to retrieve and tractability. Marking is the ability to watch a bird fall and then accurately find it. Marking can be improved with training, but a dog with a keen set of eyes and the

ability to use them is born, not made. Scenting abilities, or nose, can never be added or improved, but are inborn.

Birdiness and the desire to retrieve are genetic. A dog can be trained to retrieve and trained to pick up a bird, but training can never take the place of a dog whose entire being and every desire is directed towards the goal of retrieving a bird. This can be spotted in young puppies that become delirious with joy the first time they are introduced to a bird and pick it up without any hesitation at all.

The skills that can and must be trained require a tractable dog, and this is another inborn quality. Some dogs are born wanting to please and willing to learn. Other dogs with wonderful innate qualities are so set on doing things their way and are unwilling to learn that they can be almost useless as hunting dogs.

The learned skills include steadiness on the line until sent to retrieve and retrieving to hand and in heel position, as opposed to dropping the bird near the area of the hunter. Handling a dog to a bird it did not see fall (a blind) requires the utmost in trainability, as the dog must listen and watch the handler for directions to the bird. This is a difficult concept for a headstrong dog lacking in trainability.

FIELD TRIALS

AKC-licensed field trials began as a testing ground for the finest retrievers imported and bred in the 1930s. All dog activities were pastimes of the wealthy, but this was especially true of field trials. Almost all dogs were run by professional trainers.

Trials were originally modeled after their British counterparts, but soon took on a life and form of their own. The statement in the Field Trial Rules that says a test should simulate an average day's hunt has been ignored for decades. The gunners and throwers wear white shirts or jackets so they are visible to the dog. Marking distances are commonly 250 yards or more. Blinds may be up to 400 yards long.

Despite the fact that field trials have very little to do with hunting other than testing the skills

The desire to retrieve is evident in the speed, style and intensity of this Golden. (Sue Nelson)

required of a hunting dog, they are fun, challenging and the ultimate test of the abilities of a retriever.

FIELD TRIAL DIVISIONS

Retriever field trials are open to all retriever breeds and Irish Water Spaniels over the age of six months. There are four divisions, or stakes, held at almost all field trials: Derby, Qualifying, Amateur All-Age and Open All-Age.

Derby stakes are open to dogs under two years of age. Derby tests are meant to judge natural abilities, as opposed to trained abilities. All the tests are marking tests, usually a combination of singles, doubles and an occasional triple. Live birds are shot

A Golden returns to its handler on a land retrieve. (Cheryl Baca)

A field trial handler sends his dog on a mark. The judge observes the dog from behind the line. (Janis Teichman)

dogs that complete all of the series satisfactorily, but are not among the placements.

One of the goals for many Derby competitors is to make the National Derby List. This distinction is awarded to a dog that has earned 10 or more points in Licensed Derby Stakes. A win is worth five points; second place earns three points; third place gets two points; and fourth place earns one point. The dog that earns the most points in a year is the National Derby Champion. Over the years there have been several Golden Retrievers that have been National Derby Champs.

The Qualifying stake is the next level after Derby. In this stake, dogs are tested on a multiple land mark (a double or a triple) and a multiple

at least once, with the bird thrown and shot by assigned gunners. This is called a live gun station. Other stations will throw dead birds, with one person throwing and a second person at the same location shooting a blank load out of a gun in the direction of the thrown bird. A single is when one mark is thrown and the dog is sent to retrieve.

A double is two marks thrown in succession before the dog is sent. The dog must then retrieve each fall, one at a time. A triple is when the dog sees three birds thrown in succession before being sent.

In a Derby, dogs are judged on their efficiency in finding the bird in a quick and stylish manner. The dog that takes the straightest line to the fall and finds the birds with the least amount of hunting is awarded first place. Placements are also awarded for second through fourth. In addition, Judges Awards of Merit (JAMs) are given out to

Mo's Far-To-Go Speedy Peach, JH***, owned by Jim and Kathy Pickering, is the all-time high-point female Golden Retriever Derby winner with 54 points. (Jim Pickering)

water mark. In addition, a water blind and a land blind of easy to moderate difficulty can be expected. A blind simulates a bird that has been shot but the dog does not see fall. The handler knows where this bird is, sends the dog and uses hand signals to direct the dog to the bird. A single blast of a whistle is used to indicate to the dog that it should stop and look at the handler for another signal.

Most dogs entered in the Qualifying stake are over the age of two, but have not placed in an All-Age stake. A dog that wins or places second in a Qualifying receives All-Age status.

The Amateur All-Age is the only stake restricted to amateur handlers. Some amateur stakes are limited to owner-amateur handlers. The tests are extremely demanding. One should expect land and water triples and land and water blinds of extreme difficulty. Dogs earn points for first through fourth placements (first earns five points, second earns three points, third earns one point, fourth earns half a point). The title Amateur Field Champion (AFC) is awarded to the dog that accumulates a total of 15 points in Amateur stakes, including at least one win.

The Open All-Age stake is the most demanding and difficult offered. At many trials only qualified All-Age dogs are eligible to enter. In some parts of the country, Open stakes are almost totally dominated by professional handlers. Success at this level is very difficult for the amateur trainer and handler.

Marking tests usually consist of triples or even quadruples and the blinds are often incredibly difficult. Points are awarded in the same manner as

AFC Glenhaven Devil's Advocate, UDT, MH, WCX, sits next to the trophy and rosette from his first Amateur win. His proud breeder-trainer-handler-owner, Glenda Brown, is beside him. (Richard Brown)

the Amateur stakes. A Field Championship (FC) is earned by accumulating 10 points, of which five must be from a win. A dog that is handled by an amateur that earns 10 points in Open stakes is awarded the Amateur Field Champion (AFC) title in addition to the FC.

Field trials are extremely competitive, but very rewarding in terms of achievement. The owner of a dog that completes a field trial stake at any level should be very proud of the accomplishment.

WHAT IT TAKES TO WIN

Success in field trials requires a dog that is structurally and mentally sound. It must at least be a very good marker, and to succeed at the higher levels of competition it must have a nearly perfect balance of drive, desire and trainability. Still, the finest dog in the world will not be successful unless it receives proper training.

Training for field trials is time-consuming, requires access to a variety of land and water terrain, and is costly in terms of time, equipment, travel and entry fees. Additionally, you need the help of other people to throw birds and offer advice.

There is always room in the sport for the devoted amateur with an excellent dog and the necessary support team, but success may require the services of a professional trainer. Training fees may run as high as $500 to $600 a month. This does not include entry and handling fees.

FINDING A FIELD TRIAL

Field trials are held throughout the country from late January through early December. Before entering a field trial, it is advisable to attend one. The dates and locations are listed in the *Events Calendar* supplement to the *AKC Gazette*, and the publication *Retriever Field Trial News*. If these publications are not available, your local telephone book may have a retriever trainer or retriever club listed that

Training is hard work. This Golden is retrieving a practice bumper. (Janis Teichman)

may be able to help in locating a nearby trial. You can also inquire at local gun or sporting goods stores.

HUNTING TESTS

Before the advent of hunting tests, the only place you could really prove the field abilities of your dog was at field trials. There was no place for the average hunter or the person with a nice dog but limited resources to run their dog competitively. Success in field trials is a full-time commitment, and many people interested in working retrievers were left out in the cold.

Retriever clubs often held gun dog stakes at their picnic trials, and in some parts of the country sanctioned trials provided an outlet. Since none of these are formal events, there was no recognition for success other than a ribbon.

In the early 1980s two separate movements to form field events that would actually test the hunting abilities of retrievers and that were within the scope of the time and financial restrictions of the average hunter or retriever enthusiast took form. The Hunting Retriever Club (HRC), under the auspices of the United Kennel Club, and the North American Hunting Retriever Association (NAHRA) were formed for the purpose of conducting hunting tests. NAHRA and the American Kennel Club were originally partners, but quickly separated, with the AKC setting up its own hunt test program.

Tests held through the HRC and NAHRA are found regionally. HRC is most prevalent in the South, with a few clubs in Colorado and the Midwest. NAHRA is primarily in the Northeast, Southern California and Arizona. AKC hunt tests are the most widespread and are found uniformly throughout the country.

The similarities between the three programs are greater than the differences. The more obvious differences are that distances allowed on marks may vary. In HRC tests the handler carries a gun and fires a blank popper load in the direction of the thrown bird. NAHRA requires quartering and flushing in its upper-level tests.

WHAT'S THE DIFFERENCE BETWEEN FIELD TRIALS AND HUNT TESTS?

The most obvious difference is that all hunt test programs are non-competitive. Dogs either pass and receive a qualifying score and credit towards a hunt test title or fail and come back to try again.

The distances of marks and blinds are much shorter. In AKC tests, distances should be no more than 100 yards. This is more realistic in regard to the distances birds actually fall when shot by a hunter, but are short by field trial standards.

Gunners, throwers and handlers wear camouflage or dark clothing. Gun stations are often hidden, with the bird originating from cover or a bush or tree line. Shots are often fired from the line in the direction of the thrown bird. Calls, decoys, boats and holding blinds are used extensively, and the handler is required to carry a gun during at least a portion of the test. This gun is usually non-functional and may be nothing more than a piece of PVC pipe glued to an old gun stock.

In hunt tests, the handlers wear camouflage and carry a shotgun for at least part of the test. (Janis Teichman)

HUNT TEST LEVELS

All three hunt test programs offer three levels of testing based on the training level of the dog. The titles earned from the organizations vary, but the requirements and expectations are similar. The first level, which is called Junior in AKC tests, is designed for a young dog just starting out. Natural ability is stressed, with a dog expected to show good marking, nose and perseverance. A dog does not need to be steady, although it must be under control when held by light restraint and it must deliver the bird to hand.

At the Junior level, a dog is tested on two land singles and two water singles. When it passes four different Junior tests it is awarded the title Junior Hunter (JH).

The next level, Senior, is for dogs that have a season or two of hunting behind them. The Senior hunter is expected to be steady and honor while

A Golden waits with eagerness and intensity to be sent. (Andrea Fisher)

another dog is sent to retrieve. Double retrieves are required on land and water, and the dog must be able to do a fairly simple land blind and water blind.

This is a dog that any hunter would be proud to own. In the AKC program, a dog that receives five qualifications (four if it previously earned a Junior title) is awarded the Senior Hunter (SH) title.

The most difficult tests are for the finished retriever. The Master Hunter is the dog that can do anything. It must be able to do triples, diversion marks and multiple blinds in conjunction with marks. Its performance must be nearly flawless and faults that are overlooked at the lower levels are severely penalized or are cause for disqualification at this level.

Master-level tests include three separate tests of multiple marks on land, water and a land-water

Comstock Sunfire Tin Emeline, UD, MH***, and Windjammer Cadydid Emeline, UD, WH, are weekend hunt test qualifiers. (Mary Hilderbrandt)

combination. The Master dog must also do a land blind and water blind, which is often closely associated with marks. A dog that qualifies at six tests (five scores if it previously earned a Senior title) becomes a Master Hunter (MH) in the AKC program.

All three organizations offer further testing for the elite. The HRC offers Grand Hunts, with the ultimate goal to become Grand Hunting Retriever Champion (GRHRC). NAHRA offers regional tests that dogs must qualify for. The select few that pass these tests become Grand Master Hunting Retrievers. The AKC program showcases its finest Master Hunters through a nationally held test conducted by the Master National Retriever Club. At all levels, the tests seen at these events are generally much more difficult than those found at a weekend hunt test.

HOW TO FIND A HUNT TEST

The dates and locations of hunt tests can be found in the publications of the organizations that sponsor them. HRC tests are listed in the magazine *Hunting Retriever*. NAHRA tests are listed in the *NAHRA News*. AKC tests are listed in the *Events Calendar* and *AKC Afield*. Besides the date and location, the test secretary will be listed. This is the person to contact for information and an entry form. Entries usually must be received about a week and a half before the date of the event.

If you can't find any of these publications, try calling a retriever training kennel or a local dog club. They may know of a test or be able to refer you to someone with the necessary information.

Mark Berman and his dog Caleb approach the line on a walk-up in a Senior test. (Laurie Berman)

While the hunt test program is still young in terms of history and has problems to work out, it is growing at an amazing rate. It has brought people into the sport that would never have been attracted otherwise, and made fanciers more aware of enhancing and improving the retrieving abilities of their dogs.

STARTING A YOUNG DOG

The surest sign of a good field prospect is a puppy or dog that loves to retrieve. In a puppy this is obvious when everything that can be picked up is in its mouth and anything that is thrown is brought back. Older dogs that have had no previous exposure to field work can be successful if they have a natural love of birds and a desire to retrieve.

Early work with puppies should be fun and simple, emphasizing good traits and building confidence. Do not try to attempt too much, as many bad habits and problems can develop from expecting performance without a good foundation of early training.

Walks through all types of terrain and vegetation are a good way to accustom a dog to cover and build confidence. Introduce it to water by going in the water with the dog, make it fun and quit while they still want more.

If a bird wing or freshly killed pigeon or duck is available, introduce your dog to the bird. Toss it a few feet in front of the dog, and encourage the dog to pick it up and carry it around. Praise lavishly for its interest in the bird. If the dog starts to play with the bird and tear it up, remove it at once. You know the dog likes birds, but bad habits that can be difficult to correct are formed by allowing a puppy to be destructive with a bird.

Any marks that are thrown should be simple. If you do not have a bird or puppy bumper available, a makeshift bumper can be made by stuffing a white sock with paper. When this is thrown, make sure it is always visible so that the puppy is always

A potential field prospect must have a natural love for birds. This puppy has a pheasant wing. (Barbara Taylor)

successful. Restrict the throws to no more than three in any session, so that the puppy does not become bored and always looks forward to retrieving. If it looks like you have a real prospect, it is time to get some real equipment and find books and people that can help you and your dog.

TRAINING EQUIPMENT

The actual equipment you will need to begin field training is relatively minimal. However, it can become very expensive, depending on the goals you set and the individual needs of your dog. You will need a couple of whistles. You will want to purchase one specifically marketed for dog training, as these have a clear, piercing pitch that travels better over distances. A simple lanyard is good to hang the whistles on. You will wear the lanyard around your neck.

You will need a leash, of course, and training bumpers. Bumpers are made of a soft plastic and come in a variety of colors, with white and red being the most common. These are used for everyday training, as few people can afford to use real birds every day. A rope is tied through the hole at one end of the bumper so it can be thrown greater distances. An inexpensive training pistol that shoots small blanks is useful to accustom a dog to gunshots and creates more excitement and realism.

Retriever training books and videos are readily available, but this is one activity where hands-on help and advice is just about mandatory. It is a sport that really must be seen to be properly understood and executed.

Some retriever clubs and professional trainers offer retrieving classes. They usually meet once a week. The best way to learn is to find a mentor. This might be a knowledgeable amateur trainer or a training group. Most retriever trainers are more than happy to help a serious newcomer to the sport. The continuation of the sport depends on new blood. Free help and advice is available from

The spectacular water entry of a working Golden. Shane is diving for a practice bumper. (Laurie Berman)

most amateurs, on the condition that you are willing to go out in the field and help throw birds and bumpers for others in the training group.

Field training provides excellent exercise for the dog and owner. Attending trials and tests gives you an opportunity to see and use land areas that might never be open to the general public. Field training is also the truest test of a dog's soundness, trainability and natural instincts.

(Bill Newcomb)

CHAPTER 11

What Else Can You Do With a Golden?

Activities for Golden Retrievers are by no means limited to conformation shows and field events. A breed that is so trainable, athletic and versatile is suitable for many endeavors. The only limits are the interests and resources of the owner and participation restrictions placed by the groups that organize the events.

OBEDIENCE

There is no other activity where Goldens are so popular or dominant than obedience. The sport and the breed could be said to have been made for each other. Obedience trials test the dog and handler on a series of exercises that are designed to show teamwork, trainability and the usefulness of a dog in responding to commands. The Golden, with its happy attitude, stylish manner and good looks, makes an ideal competitor.

Obedience is a sport that is within the scope of the abilities and resources of almost every Golden owner. A Golden from any background (from show to field to backyard bred) can do well, and it can be of any size, color or type. The only requirement is that it is AKC-registered and physically capable of work.

Correct movement is important for a Golden, regardless of the type of work it is performing. (June Smith)

Obedience trials test three levels of training: Novice, Open and Utility. Novice exercises are based upon the everyday skills a dog needs to be a well-behaved companion. This is reflected in the title Companion Dog (CD), which a dog earns upon receiving three qualifying scores. A Novice-level dog is tested on heeling on and off leash. The heel on leash includes moving in a figure-eight pattern around two people. The stand for examination indicates that a dog will allow a stranger to touch it without exhibiting fear or aggressiveness. The final individual exercise is the recall, where the dog is called from a sitting position on the other side of the ring and must come and sit in front of the handler (called the front), then go to heel position (the finish) on command.

Finally, a Novice dog must do a one-minute sit-stay and a three-minute down-stay, off leash with other dogs on both sides of it (called the group exercise), while the handler is at the other end of the ring.

Points are deducted for minor errors. Serious errors, such as leaving the ring at any time, not coming on the recall, or getting up on the stay exercises receive an automatic zero and a non-qualifying score. When all the points are added up, a total score of at least 170 is required to pass. Dogs that pass receive a qualifying ribbon, and the four dogs with the highest scores receive first through fourth place.

The Open level requires basic obedience skills, along with athletic and

Hickory Dickory Zachary, UDT, JH, WCX, clears the high jump with the dumbbell. (Andrea Johnson)

Am./Can. Ch. Cobrador's Hijo de Espana, CD, goes airborne on the broad jump. (Jane Bailey)

The broad jump landing. (Andrea Johnson)

retrieving abilities. All exercises are performed off leash. Initially, a dog must heel off leash. This is followed by the drop on recall, where a dog is called by the handler and commanded to drop at the signal of the judge.

Then the dog must retrieve a dumbbell on flat ground, retrieve the same dumbbell over a high jump by going out and back over the jump and finish by cleanly clearing the broad jump.

The group exercise at the Open level consists of a three-minute sit-stay and five-minute down-stay with the handlers out of sight. Minor deductions are for heeling errors, crooked fronts and finishes and slow responses to commands. A dog is disqualified for any of the errors mentioned in the Novice section, plus failures to jump or retrieve. Again, three qualifying scores are required for the Companion Dog Excellent (CDX) title.

The most difficult level is Utility. In addition to the skills previously tested, a dog must be able to pay absolute attention by following hand signals and use its scenting abilities. The heeling exercise is off leash and done without any verbal commands, only hand signals. At the completion of the heeling exercise, the dog is left in a stand-stay while the handler walks to the end of the ring. The dog is then commanded by hand signals only to down, sit and come.

Scent discrimination follows, with the handler touching two objects (scent articles) from among 10. The scent articles consist of five metal and five leather objects that are identical in size and appearance. These are placed about 20 feet from the dog and handler, and with the working team facing the opposite direction, one of the scented articles is placed among the eight that have been scented by the judge. The dog is then sent to find the article with its handler's scent. This is repeated with the other selected article.

In the directed retrieve, the dog must retrieve one of three gloves placed in each corner of the ring and in the far end. The dog is sent from the middle of the ring. The handler and dog must turn and line up in the direction of the glove they have

Flying over the bar jump in a directed jump. (American Kennel Club)

been told to retrieve by the judge, and then the handler sends the dog to the correct glove.

A bar jump and a high jump are used in the directed jumping exercise. The dog is sent to the other end of the ring between the two jumps, commanded to sit and then by arm and/or verbal signal told to jump over either the bar or the high

jump. There is no group exercise, but a stand followed by a recall is the final exercise.

It is obvious that there are many reasons for a dog to fail a Utility test. Inability to follow signals, returning with an incorrect scent article or the wrong glove, failure to jump or take the correct jump are all reasons for a non-qualifying score, besides all of the disqualifications applicable to Novice and Open. A dog that receives three hard-earned qualifying scores earns the Utility Dog (UD) title.

Obedience competition does not have to end when a dog gets its UD. Obedience is both a non-competitive and a competitive sport. You can enter with the sole intention of earning qualifying scores and titles, or your goal can be getting the highest scores. The dog with the highest score of all three levels in the A and B divisions (classes are divided into A and B, depending on the handler's previous experience in Novice or whether a dog has earned a CDX or UD in Open and Utility) is awarded the High in Trial. First and second placements in Open B and Utility B count towards points for an Obedience Trial Championship (OTCh). A dog that has earned the Utility Dog title and has a minimum of 100 points in Open and Utility competition, with at least one win in both, becomes an OTCh.

Another non-competitive obedience title was added in the mid-1990s. This is the Utility Dog Excellent (UDX), and recognizes consistency in qualifying in both Open and Utility. To be eligible a dog must be a UD, and then receive qualifying scores in both Open and Utility at the same trial on 10 different occasions.

Obedience trials are held somewhere in the country almost every weekend of the year. They are held in conjunction with many conformation shows and also as separate trials. The dates and locations can be found in the *Events Calendar* supplement to the *AKC Gazette*. In addition, most local obedience schools or clubs will know about upcoming trials.

No one should ever enter the obedience ring without reading a copy of the rule book. Single copies can be obtained at no charge from the AKC. If there are doubts about the interpretation of the rules, ask questions.

Getting Started in Obedience

The simplest way to begin obedience training, whether the goal is a well-behaved pet or a title, is to attend a basic obedience class. The curriculum of most obedience classes is based on Novice obedience exercises. The required rules and precision may not be stressed, but the basics should prepare you for future training.

Dog obedience classes are held nearly everywhere. They may be offered by town recreation departments, private professional trainers, dog clubs and even animal shelters. There are no qualifications for an obedience instructor, so it is wise to ask for recommendations, inquire about qualifications and observe classes before actually enrolling your dog and yourself. If you are specifically interested in obedience competition, the instructor should have actual competition experience and should have put advanced titles on a dog.

Another good qualification is membership in the National Association of Dog Obedience Instructors (NADOI). This is a group of dedicated dog instructors who are accepted into the organization under strict conditions. There are a number of schools for dog trainers that turn out 30-day graduates. Avoid trainers with these "qualifications." The ability to train dogs, and to teach others how to train their dogs, is a skill that requires a special knack and years of experience.

Obedience Equipment

At the Novice level the expenses and equipment involved are minimal. You need only a six-foot leash and a training collar. Traditionally a slip collar made of chain (sometimes called a choke chain, although the idea is never to choke the dog) is most often used. The choke chain is the only collar accepted in competition. It should only be worn when the dog is being trained or under the direct supervision of its owner.

Some people prefer to train with a pinch collar. This has several other common names, such as prong or spike collar. It is made of a series of interconnected links that have metal points that rest directly on the surface of the dog's neck. They are useful for someone with little strength and a physically strong dog. Many people consider their use to be more humane than a choke chain, as the precise timing required for proper corrections on a choke chain are not required with a prong collar.

Dogs can be nagged and improperly trained with either one of these collars. The decision is usually made with the advice of a training instructor and the individual needs of the dog and handler.

Training can be done in your house, yard or local park or school grounds. Any place that allows dogs is a good location to train and accustom the dog to responding in all kinds of situations with all sorts of distractions. The time you need to spend depends on the level of competition you wish to attain. The perfection needed for high scores

You'll need wooden dumbbells to train for the more advanced levels. Make sure you buy ones that are the right size for your dog's mouth. (American Kennel Club)

requires time and preparation. Less lofty goals can be met with 20-minute sessions several times a week.

As training advances, more time and equipment is involved. Obedience jumps can be made for the cost of wood and a can of paint. Relatively inexpensive plastic jump sets can be purchased that are lightweight and easily transported for training in various locations.

Obedience is accessible to everyone and has useful applications in everyday life with a dog. The relationship you will develop with your dog from hours of training, travel and ring experience cannot be equaled, nor can the feeling of pride and accomplishment that comes with earning an obedience title.

THE CANINE GOOD CITIZEN PROGRAM

The American Kennel Club devised the Canine Good Citizen (CGC) program in the 1980s to help promote responsible dog ownership. It is open to dogs of any breed, mixed or purebred. The tests are simple and are designed to show that a dog is well behaved, a pleasure to live with and has proper temperament. If obedience competition is not your cup of tea but you'd still like some recognition that you have a well-mannered dog, CGC is for you.

There are 10 tests a dog must pass. The dog must allow a friendly stranger to approach and speak to the handler. The dog should sit on command and allow a stranger to pet it. The dog is then touched and brushed or combed by the evaluator. The dog must walk on a loose leash and be able to walk through a crowd. Then it must demonstrate that it can sit or down in place at the end of a 12-foot line. When the dog is praised, it must be able to calm down quickly. Interaction with other dogs is tested when two dogs approach each other, their handlers greet each other and continue on their way. The dogs should show no more than a slight interest in each other. Mental stability is tested by an action or occurrence that is unusual or surprising; this might be a loud sound, a dropped object or the sudden motion of a stranger. The dog is then tied on a long line and left under supervision; it must not display undue distress.

Extensive training is not required to pass a CGC test. The skills learned in a basic obedience class should be sufficient. CGC tests are commonly offered at conformation and obedience matches, though they may be held as individual events. A dog that passes all 10 parts of the test receives a certificate that states the dog is a Canine Good Citizen.

TEMPERAMENT TESTS

American Temperament Test Society (ATTS) has developed a test similar in concept to the CGC, with temperament as the focus rather than obedience. During a temperament test, a dog is exposed to a variety of conditions it might encounter in everyday life. These might include people exhibiting a variety of behaviors, sounds, and loud and strange environments. A dog is critiqued based on its reactions to these stimuli. A dog that passes receives a certificate and the title TT.

TRACKING

Tracking is another pursuit in which Goldens excel. Their strong scenting abilities make them outstanding trackers. Becoming involved in tracking can be more difficult, not because Goldens lack anything, but because there are fewer people involved in the sport than in obedience or field training. There are some excellent books on the topic, but hands-on help is almost essential.

There are three levels of tracking proficiency recognized by the AKC, and a single passing score at a trial is required to earn any title. The titles are

This young Golden has found the glove. (Susie Rezy)

Tracking Dog (TD), Tracking Dog Excellent (TDX) and Variable Surface Tracker (VST). A dog that has earned all three titles is awarded the title Champion Tracker (CT). Even though all tracking titles are non-competitive, the CT title is placed in front of the dog's registered name.

The essential feature of all tracking tests is that the dog must follow the scent of a stranger and find the articles they have left on the track. The differences in what is expected at the three levels are based on the dog's age, length and complexity of the track and the number of articles that must be found.

At the TD level, a track is no more than 30 minutes old and about 440 yards long with two right-hand turns and one object to find. The TDX track is about two hours old, about 800 yards long, has cross-tracks of other scents, four objects to find throughout the track and multiple turns. The terrain and conditions found on the TDX track are varied and one can expect a variety of changes.

The VST track is 600 to 800 yards long and from one and a half to three and a half hours old in an urban environment. Tracks can be laid next to buildings, through or along fences and over any surface a person might go, within the safety limits of the dog. Turns are on different surfaces with at least one on a surface that has no vegetation. The dog must find and retrieve four objects dropped on the track—one is made of leather, one of plastic, one of metal and one of fabric. There is one starting flag at the beginning of the track, but no others.

At all levels, the handler walks the track with the dog in harness, but has no idea where the track goes and must totally trust their dog. Dogs may be spoken to and encouraged verbally at all tracking levels, and there are no time limits as long as the dog is working.

Tracking Equipment

The essential needs of the tracking enthusiast include a harness made of leather or webbed nylon that the dog wears while working, and a tracking line that is between 20 and 40 feet long. You may want to make or purchase small flags or some type of marker to indicate the track.

Tracking requires the help of other people to lay tracks, and access to land where practice tracks can be set up. At the early stages small areas are sufficient, but as training progresses larger areas that offer a variety of distractions are needed.

Getting Started

Dogs can be started on tracking when they are very young; tracking is actually more of a game than formal training to a young dog. Goldens have been known to earn their tracking degrees shortly after six months of age.

Some basic commands are needed before starting, such as sit and come. The prospective tracker must also be able to pick up and retrieve an object. There are many methods used to teach a dog to track, but at the early stages tracks should be short, simple and straight.

Before entering your first tracking test, a letter is required certifying that the dog is ready to track. This can be obtained from a tracking judge who sets up a simple, informal track. The number of people entered in each tracking test is limited, and to make sure that all dogs have a fair chance at entering tests and passing, this preliminary screening is necessary.

A tracking rule book can be obtained by writing to the AKC.

AGILITY

Agility is a young and quickly growing dog sport. It came to this country in 1986 from Britain, where it originated as an exhibition sport that somewhat resembles show jumping for horses. It combines obedience with athleticism, accuracy and speed.

Agility is basically a canine obstacle course, and the obstacles might include various jumps, A-frame, seesaw, pause table, dog walk, rigid tunnel, tire, collapsed tunnel and weave poles.

Four organizations currently offer agility competitions and titles in the United States: the American Kennel Club, the United Kennel Club

Emberain Pacific Storm, UD, JH, MX, WCX, on the dog walk. Handler and dog run an agility course at full speed. (Bill Newcomb)

(UKC), the North American Dog Agility Council (NADAC) and the United States Dog Agility Association (USDAA). The specific rules can be obtained by writing to each organization. The basic rules are the same, with the differences being the height of jumps and the size of contact zones (areas a dog must touch as it enters and exits each obstacle).

Contact zones exist for the safety of the dog, rather than as a way for a dog to fail. If these margins of safety did not exist, dogs would be allowed to jump from heights and risk injury in a sport that is already demanding in its requirements for soundness and athleticism.

Scores and placements in AKC tests are based on a combination of the point total (100 is perfect) and the time it took to complete the course. Agility resembles obedience in that it offers satisfaction for both the competitive and non-competitive handler. Each level is divided into height divisions, so that dogs compete against dogs of similar height. Goldens are in the 20-inch or 24-inch division. The top four performances at each height level get an award, and non-placing qualifiers earn legs towards titles.

In AKC competitions, three qualifying scores of 85 or more are required to earn an Agility title. The three AKC levels, and their respective titles, are Novice Agility (NA), Open Agility (OA) and Agility Excellent (AX). A dog with an AX title that earns three more qualifying scores at this level earns the title of Master Agility Excellent (MX).

The differences in the three levels are the number of obstacles and their placement in relationship to each other. The course is set up by the

Emberain Jelly's First Jam, CDX, JH, AX, WCX, sails through the tire. (Bill Newcomb)

judge and a maximum course time is set. The time is based on the length of the course and number of obstacles. The handlers are allowed to view the course before the start of competition. Missing an obstacle, taking obstacles in the wrong order, missing a contact zone or exceeding the course time all incur penalties.

Sunfire Second Wind Scout, CD, JH, WCX, climbs over the A-frame. (Susan Stewart)

offer lessons and have the proper equipment. Agility equipment can be purchased or made, but it requires room and is not easily moved.

Agility provides excellent training and exercise for a soundly put together Golden. It builds a dog's confidence and understanding of its body. It is also excellent exercise for the handler, as they must race around the course to give directions to the dog. Most of all, agility is fast and fun and builds a real sense of teamwork.

Getting Started in Agility

Agility is not a sport for very young or very old dogs. A dog should be fully mature physically (at least two years old) before it begins serious agility training. The stress encountered in this type of training can be extremely harmful to growing bones. A puppy can be introduced to certain pieces of equipment, such as the tunnel and the walks, with supervision. But any jumping should only be done with the jumps flat on the ground, so the puppy only associates the word jump with the act of going over an object.

Certain obedience skills are necessary. A dog must be able to do sit-stays and down-stays for the pause table, and to prevent it from jumping off of equipment. It must know "come" and be able to heel off leash.

For anyone just getting started, it is probably best to find an agility club or trainer. They will

Emberain Jelly's First Jam, CDX, JH, AX, WCX, works the weave poles. This exercise requires precision, athletic ability and teamwork. (Bill Newcomb)

FLYBALL

Flyball is another activity that combines several skills, plus a dog's sense of fun. Organized competition is offered through the North American Flyball Association. It is truly a team sport, as you and your dog will be competing on a team with other handlers and dogs, and integrates athletic ability and a love of retrieving.

A flyball team is made up of four dogs and four handlers. The dogs compete relay style, jumping over a series of hurdles. At the end of the hurdles, they must press a lever on a box that tosses a ball into the air. The dog must catch the ball and return over the hurdles to its handler. Then the next dog on the team goes. The team with the fastest total time wins.

Jumps and a flyball box are required, as is a good supply of tennis balls. Since this is a team sport, team members and their dogs are also needed. Titles are offered and earned by winning points.

SEARCH AND RESCUE

Search and rescue is not an activity for most dog fanciers. There is no recognition or titles to be earned. The work requires extensive training and is physically demanding. But for those up to the challenge, it can be immensely rewarding.

Search and rescue encompasses a variety of skills, and many dogs are specially trained to perform certain types of rescue. Golden Retrievers are excellent candidates for search and rescue dogs, as they possess most of the required characteristics. A search and rescue dog should be intelligent, have stamina, have a high play drive, be curious, demanding of attention, get along well with other dogs, love other people, love to dig, love to travel in cars, not be interested in chasing games and be unafraid of heights and water.

Training a dog to "call out" status (the point when they are ready to work) takes between 18 months and two years. As dogs are usually retired at the age of eight, it is best to start a dog as a puppy. Initial training should be fun, where finding a person is a game of hide and seek. A potential rescue dog must be proficient in the basic obedience skills of heeling off leash, coming when called, long sits and downs with the handler out of sight and directed send-outs of up to 25 yards.

A dog must be able to complete an agility course, which should include a bridge, climbing or balancing on a rock or slide area, going through a tunnel and crawling under an obstacle. The dog must be able to swim at least 50 feet. The dog must be willing to enter a vehicle with its handler and four or five other dogs, and show no signs of aggression or fear.

This does not even touch on the actual training involved in learning to scent. Most search and rescue organizations use dogs trained in air scenting (as opposed to the ground scenting used in tracking competition). This is almost always done off lead with the dog searching up to a quarter mile ahead of the handler. The dog is attempting to locate a person's scent cone in order to locate them. Once the victim is located, the dog returns to the handler and alerts them of the find. The command "show me" is then given, and the dog returns to the victim.

Traditional tracking is not effective in actual search and rescue. Search and rescue dogs are more correctly termed trailers, as they use a combination of tracking and air scenting skills.

Dogs are used by search and rescue agencies in all kinds of searches. These include wilderness, water recovery, avalanche, cadaver, evidence and urban disaster. Dogs can be cross-trained, but training in one area should be complete before another area is started, or it can lead to confusion.

The handler must be equally qualified, and anyone interested in this activity should be physically fit. They must take CPR and first aid courses and be proficient in the use of maps and a compass.

Search and rescue is not a paid position—it is done by volunteers. You must be able to pay for all of the expenses involved with training, transportation, equipment and uniforms (although when you are sent to a disaster site, your way will usually be paid by another agency). Training must be done regularly, and team members usually meet weekly.

The Golden is a perfect candidate for this worthy form of employment, but it takes total commitment on the part of the owner. There are many search and rescue organizations throughout the country. The address of the national organization is listed in Appendix A.

THERAPY DOGS

One of the most wonderful aspects of owning a dog is the emotional comfort and support they provide. These qualities are even more in evidence when dogs are used as a form of therapy in the treatment of disturbed, ill and older people. Goldens are ideal for this activity, with their gentle, loving temperaments, expressive eyes and coats that invite hands to touch and stroke. A visit with a well-behaved Golden can be more helpful in a patient's recovery than any medication, or make the day of someone in confinement. The dog makes no judgments, asks for nothing and only gives love and comfort.

There is more to volunteer therapy dog work than visiting an old folks' home with a dog when the time and mood is right. There are several organizations that certify dogs as suitable for therapy work. The best known of these are the Delta

Am./Can. Ch. Cobrador's Acapulco, CD, TT, CGC, sharing his Golden personality and charm at a United Cerebral Palsy center. (Jane Bailey)

Society, Therapy Dogs Incorporated and Therapy Dogs International. Dogs used for this work must be well-behaved and usually must have a Canine Good Citizen certificate.

Training to familiarize a dog with the things it may encounter, such as the noise of metal pans, strange odors, wheelchairs and medical equipment, is a part of the preparation. The dog must never jump on people and must be trained in proper etiquette, such as the gentle placement of front paws. The dog must then pass an examination given by a tester certified by the organization. A dog that passes receives the right to use the title Therapy Dog.

Polo at work as a therapy dog. (Tom Bailey)

The rewards of therapy work are in the heart and knowing that your dog is helping others who are not lucky enough to have a dog of their own.

GUIDE AND ASSISTANCE DOGS

No discussion of the many things Golden Retrievers can do would be complete without mentioning the many aspects of the Golden's role in helping the disabled. While training an assistance dog is not something the average dog owner can do, this role is a vital one for the breed.

Golden Retrievers were first used as guides for the blind. There are a number of schools that teach

Owning a therapy dog requires commitment on the part of the owner. The work is often more difficult for the owner than the dog, as many people cannot confront illness with such regularity. Routine visits are scheduled at care facilities, and the routine must be strictly followed. People come to depend on such visits and letting them down may cause a breakdown in their care and recovery.

dogs and owners how to work as a team, but the first and most famous is Guide Dogs for the Blind, with its headquarters in California.

This organization has been followed by Canine Companions for Independence, Hearing Dogs for the Deaf and countless other groups that train dogs to help make the lives of the disabled easier. It is the natural retrieving instincts that make Goldens so

A working Golden trained and provided by Canine Companions for Independence. (Joanne A. Gaulke)

ideal for much of this work, whether it is to turn on light switches, open doors or pick up the telephone.

Many of these organizations have strict requirements for the dogs that are bred or donated for training. The working dog must be sound in body and completely sound in temperament. Other organizations will accept a rescued dog that appears to have the necessary attributes.

You can get involved in an assistance dog program by volunteering to raise a puppy until it reaches training age. You may also donate quality puppies or the services of your stud dog, if he would be a benefit and credit to the program.

There is no end to the many activities a Golden Retriever and its owner can become involved in. Goldens have been used as sled dogs, in beginning Schutzhund work and could probably even herd, course and dig for rats, given the right interest and training. But the basic traits inherent in a retriever give us plenty to work on without delving into the activities better associated with other breeds.

A Golden that is trained regularly and given a regular job is healthier and happy and feels it has a purpose in life. Our lives and theirs are enriched by such activities.

(Rhonda Hovan)

CHAPTER 12

The Headliners

There are so many outstanding and talented Golden Retrievers that trying to single out a handful is extremely difficult. The dogs I will focus on have been extremely successful in field, conformation or obedience competition, and most have made an impact on the Golden breed in their ability to produce outstanding offspring. Many of these dogs are the fulfillment of a breeder's dream, and all are once-in-a-lifetime dogs (The asterisks after a title denote field trial placements. For more on what they mean, see Appendix C.)

HEADLINERS IN THE FIELD

AFC Glenhaven Devil's Advocate, UDT, MH***, WCX, (OS/FDHF)

> *Sire: Smoke'n Red Apache*** (OS)*
> *Dam: OTCh Meadowpond Especial One, TD, SH, WCX, (OD/OBHF)*
> *Whelped: December 14, 1984*
> *Owner: Glenda Brown, Santa Barbara, California*

Luke was bred, owned and trained by his breeder, Glenda Brown. Her original interest in dog work was obedience, as Luke's dam, Sprite, was a High in Trial and *Dog World* Award winner. But Brown was becoming increasingly interested in field work, so she at least had hunt test titles in mind.

Luke earned his TD at 13 months of age, at the first tracking test he was entered in. She entered him in the Derby at the 1986 GRCA National Specialty Field Trial and he placed fourth. She knew she had something then, and he quickly progressed to Qualifying and achieved All-Age status with two first places. His 44.5 All-Age points include four Amateur wins.

He was retired after 1995, but qualified for two National Amateur Championships and is in the GRCA Field Dog Hall of Fame. Luke was active in hunt tests during his early years and was the first Golden Retriever in the country to earn all three AKC hunt test titles and the second Golden Master Hunter on the West Coast.

After four and a half years of going directly to heel position, he pursued his obedience career. This was to fill up the weekends when there were no field events. He earned his Companion Dog title with two firsts and one second place and scores of 198, 199 and 198.5! A year later he was a Utility Dog. His owner admits that his formal obedience training was embarrassingly limited. Luke is the first Golden with a UD title in the Field Dog Hall of Fame.

Luke is a remarkable dog, but he has had the benefit of having an outstanding owner, trainer and handler. He has been completely owner-amateur trained to all of his titles. Their success was the result of hours of dedication and hard work. The time is never worth spending unless a dog has outstanding natural ability and the desire to please, which describes Luke perfectly.

He is a GRCA Outstanding Sire and has produced Obedience Trial Champions, qualified All-Age field dogs, Master Hunters and search and rescue dogs. He has also sired many dogs that are multi-titled in field, obedience and agility. He produces a very intelligent puppy that is stylish and easy for an amateur to train. His pups have high energy without being hyperactive and are easy to live with.

Glenhaven Devil's Advocate has been successful at everything he's attempted. Completely owner-amateur trained and handled, he has produced trainable offspring in all areas of performance. (Richard Brown)

FTCh-AFTCh Shurmark's Split Decision, MH, Am.***, (OS)

Sire: FTCh-AFTCh Mioak's Shake'N Jake***, (American)

Shurmark's Split Decision is the rare field Golden that has made an impact in both the U.S. and Canada. (Mike Ducross)

Dam: Sun Fire Sure Mark Tess***, (Canadian)
Whelped: November 7, 1986
Owners: Mike and Val Ducross, Maxville, Ontario, Canada

Sprint is the rare Golden field dog that has been used as much by Canadian breeders as by Americans. His first success was as a Junior Dog (the Canadian equivalent of Derby), as he compiled 48.5 points and was the second high point overall for 1988 and the top Golden Junior Dog. He became qualified All-Age the following year, and finished his Canadian Field and Amateur Field Trial Championships in 1990.

He has qualified for numerous Canadian National Open and Amateur trials and completed nine out of 10 series at the 1991 Canadian National Open.

In 1992 he began spending winters in the U.S. under the tutelage of professional trainers Felix Mock and Dave Thompson, in an attempt to become pointed in this country. He became qualified All-Age, but time always seemed to run out before he could go further. He became an AKC Master Hunter in 1994 and was recognized by the GRCA as an Outstanding Sire in 1995.

Sprint has produced two Canadian Field Trial Champions, one of which is also an American Field Champion, as well as two Canadian Amateur Field Trial Champions. He has sired 13 qualified

Sprint's favorite activity, after lying by the fire, is hunting. (Mike Ducross)

All-Age offspring to date, several on the National Derby List and many Master and Senior Hunters.

Sprint is of Canadian breeding, though his genetic background is American Field Trial dogs. Both of his grand-sires were Field Champions in this country. He is linebred on the great producer AFC Wild Fire of Riverview CDX, WCX.

Sprint is a talented dog and is exciting to watch run. He is especially known for his courage in water. He has the ability to bounce back from corrections during training and maintains his sense of humor. He has the perfect Golden temperament, as he is biddable and loves everyone, even other dogs. He is an ideal house pet and companion. When not lying in his favorite chair by the fireplace, his favorite activity is hunting.

FC-AFC Stony-Brooks' Jersey Devil (OS/FDHF)

Sire: AFC Yankee's Smoke'N Red Devil, (OS)
Dam: Stony-Brooks' Fools Gold***, (OD)
Whelped: April 7, 1984
Owners: Bob and Marge Meegan, Overland, Kansas, and Jackie Mertens, Elgin, Illinois

Devil was bred and originally owned by Carol Lilenfeld. She did much of his early training, though Mike Lardy completed his basic training. He had nine Derby points, including a win, when he was sold to the Meegans at 18 months of age.

He made the National Derby List with 21 points and won a Qualifying while he was still a Derby dog. He spent the next five years in training with either Mike Lardy or Bill Eckett, and quickly earned both Field Championships.

Devil being sent on a mark at the National Amateur Field Trial in 1992. (Jackie Mertens)

In 1991 Bob Meegan approached Jackie Mertens about a co-ownership. Devil continued to run under Jackie and was a finalist at the 1992 National Amateur. During his career he accumulated at least 70 All-Age points.

Devil was a joy to train and run. He has a great temperament, and part of his job was as goodwill ambassador for the Golden breed. As of this writing he is still alive and is spending his retirement at Lisa and Jerry Halcomb's Sun Dance Kennel near Champaign, Illinois. He spends his time romping and swimming in the farm ponds.

Devil has sired several pointed All-Age offspring, Derby List Goldens and many Master and Senior Hunters.

Wraith's Duncan is the prepotent sire of working Goldens in field and obedience. (Dave Bluford)

Stony-Brooks' Jersey Devil accumulated 70 All-Age points and was a National Amateur finalist. (Jackie Mertens)

Wraith's Duncan, MH***, (OS)

Sire: NAFC-FC Topbrass Cotton
*Dam: Emberain Lady Nell, CD***, (OD)*
Whelped: October 14, 1984
Owners: Charles and Rosita Wraith, Alamo, California

Dogs that are outstanding performers are not always great producers. On the other hand, there are dogs that never complete their Field Championship that are outstanding producers. Unfortunately, few breeders take the time to discover these unlikely gems. It is lucky for the Golden Retriever breed that a few fanciers saw past the lack of a title and understood the natural ability of Wraith's Duncan.

Duncan did not have a notable Derby career. However, he became a qualified All-Age dog before he was two-and-a-half years old, thanks to his great marking and ability to line blinds, because it could safely be said that he could barely handle. His All-Age career included five second places, including two Open seconds. He had the required number of points for his AFC, but never won a trial.

Duncan's strength is that he is a completely natural dog. He was trained by his co-owner, Rosita Wraith, with occasional help from a professional trainer. He was never really force trained—all marking, lining and water skills were inherent.

When he is in the field, his desire to retrieve encompasses his entire being and concentration. It is because of his great intelligence, willingness to please and high retention of learned skills that it was possible for his amateur trainers to be as successful as they were. At home he is the perfect companion. He sleeps in the bedroom, sits in chairs and baby-sits the grandchildren.

As a producer, Duncan is carrying on the tradition of his sire Cotton and grand sire AFC Holway Barty in the ability to produce stylish, trainable Goldens with exceptional marking ability and desire to retrieve. To date, two of his offspring have won Amateur stakes, and many are pointed or qualified All-Age in the U.S. and Canada. He has sired over six that have made the National Derby List and as many that missed it by one point. He has produced Master and Senior Hunters, two Obedience Trial Champions and High in Trial winners.

OBEDIENCE HEADLINERS

OTCh Altair's Sardaukar Sadie, (OD/OBHF)

Sire: Ch. Sun Dance Destiny's Echo, CDX, (OS)
Dam: Meadowpond Cherokee Sunday, UDT, WC, (OD)
Whelped: November 13, 1981
Owner: Michael MacDonald, Broadview Heights, Ohio

Sadie was the one-in-a-million dog that all obedience trainers look for, and was more than a complete beginner in the sport of obedience could ever hope for. She was purchased by her owner at 18 months of age and went from Novice A to her Obedience Trial Championship in another 18 months.

Her 10-year obedience career included 84 Highs in Trial, 1,906 lifetime OTCh points and three perfect scores of 200. She had 13 placements in SuperDog and TopDog Divisions. She was nationally ranked for nine years and, as of 1997, is still the top Golden female in the AKC's Lifetime OTCh Dog Ratings. Sadie was never retired from the obedience ring, as she loved competition so much.

Altair's Sardaukar Sadie at one of her 13 placements in SuperDog or TopDog competitions. (J & J Photography)

Sadie flies over the high jump in Open competition. (Michael MacDonald)

Sadie was small and compact with a sweet personality. She often smiled at the crowd while she was performing. As amazing as her trial record is, the fact that she became a GRCA Outstanding Dam even though she only had one litter is even more amazing. In 1986 she was bred to OTCh. Meadowpond Stardust Reggie and produced eight puppies. Five of these have become Obedience Trial Champions, and four are in the Hall of Fame. Another is a CDX, WCX and Outstanding Dam and another is a UD. Her puppies have earned over 120 accumulated High in Trial awards.

OTCh. Locknor B Fifty-Two Bomber, (OS/OBHF)

> Sire: OTCh. Meadowpond Stardust Reggie, (OS/OBHF)
> Dam: OTCh. Wynwood Two Double Zera, UDTX, (OD)
> Whelped: September 18, 1984
> Owner: Nancy Patton, Lilburn, Georgia

Bomber has had an incredible obedience career that spanned nearly a decade. He earned his CD at one-and-a-half years and completed his UD a year later. By this time, he already had over 16 Highs in Trial and was in the Obedience Hall of Fame. He has had 145 HITs, three perfect scores and 75 High Combined Awards. He is ninth in all-time top OTCh dogs with 2,689 lifetime points.

His most outstanding year was 1991, when he was ranked number one by both the Whitehead High Combined Ranking System and the First and Foremost Ranking System. He was also the Ken L Ration Obedience Dog of the Year. That

Locknor B Fifty-Two Bomber with his owner, Nancy Patton. Their phenomenal success is the result of talent, training and a very special relationship. (Nancy Patton)

same year he was High in Trial at the GRCA National Specialty and received the Toby Trigger Trophy. He was an Open Gaines Classic Winner and won two SuperDog titles at Gaines Regionals.

As a producer, Bomber has sired eight Obedience Trial Champions to date.

HEADLINERS IN CONFORMATION

Ch. Elysian's Lil Leica Reprint, UDT, MH, WCX, VCX, (OD/SDHF)

Sire: Ch. Wingwathcher Reddi To Rally, CDX, WC, (OS)
Dam: Ch. Beaulieu's Akacia O'Darnley, UDT, JH, WCX, (OD)
Whelped: November 11, 1989
Owner: Jeanne von Barby, Evergreen, Colorado

Golden Retrievers can do it all, and Leica is a perfect example of a bitch that knew what was expected of her and loved every minute of it. She was worked in field and obedience at the same time she was shown in the breed ring. She was shown by her breeder-owner Jeanne von Barby, and completed her Championship from the Puppy and Bred-by-Exhibitor classes. Leica was specialed (shown as a Champion) on a limited basis and has one Best in Show and four specialty Best of Breed wins.

Her owner had never trained a Golden in the field past Junior Hunter level, but with the help and encouragement of friends, they muddled their way through Senior and completed her Master title. Leica is the only Best in Show winning Master Hunter of any sporting breed. Her field training was all based on heart and a willingness to please.

Elysian's Lil Leica Reprint is shown with her breeder and owner. She has over 60 Show Hall of Fame points, including a Best in Show win. (Bergman Photo)

Leica is the only Best in Show winner that is also a Master Hunter. (Leslie Dickerson)

The day after Leica finished her Championship, she tied for High in Trial in obedience. She is one of those dogs that comes out of the ring wondering what they can do next for entertainment.

Versatility appears to be a family trait. Leica was from a litter of four that, as grown dogs, have three Championships, two Master Hunter titles, two UDs and one TDX among them. Leica's equally famous brother is Ch. Elysian's Sky Hi Dubl Exposure, UDT, MH**, WCX, VCX, (OS).

She is not a big producer, but the puppies she has produced are similar to their dam in their ability to do anything that is asked of them. Leica is still enjoying life at nearly 10 years of age. Her love of life and willingness to please is now apparent in her grandkids.

Ch. Faera's Future Classic, (OS)

Sire: Ch. Asterling's Buster Keaton, (OS)
Dam: Ch. Faera's Puppy Kidd, (OD)
Whelped: January 31, 1990
Owner: Rhonda and Michael Hovan, Akron, Ohio

There are many top show winning dogs, but few can match Thunder in their ability to produce outstanding Goldens. Thunder started his show career by taking Reserve Winners Dog at the 1990 GRCA National Specialty at seven months of age. He competed almost exclusively from the Puppy classes, where he won both majors and Best of Breed over Group winners.

He was breeder-owner handled by the Hovans to all of his points. A specials career was never pursued, other than local shows and specialties.

It is a credit to the breeders around the country that they recognized what he has to offer without the need to be dazzled by a big winning show record. Through 1997, Thunder has produced 59 Champions with many Best in Show winners and Show Dog Hall of Fame members.

Thunder is known for producing Goldens with good health, soundness and temperament. He

Faera's Future Classic is the sire of more than 59 Champions, Best in Show winners and Show Dog Hall of Fame members. (Rhonda Hovan)

has an excellent record in terms of contributing sound hips, elbows, eyes, hearts and skin to the gene pool. Thunder is a Select Sire for several service dog organizations, including Leader Dogs for the Blind and Canine Companions for Independence.

The basis for this genetic prepotency is not an accident. His grandam was the top producing bitch in breed history, Am./Can. Ch. Amberac's Asterling Aruba, (OD/SDHF). His sire and his uncle, Ch. Asterling Go Getm Gangbuster, (OS/SDHF), have produced close to 200 Champions between them.

Thunder's older brother, the Best in Show winner Ch. Faera's Destiny Kodiak Kidd, (OS/SDHF), is an outstanding sire in his own right. Their sister, Ch. Faera's the Keepsake Kidd, (OD), is the dam of 12 Champions, two of which are Best in Show winners and three of which are in the Show Dog Hall of Fame.

Am./Can. Ch. Rush Hill's Haagen-Dazs, CDX, NA, NAJ, JH, WCX, VCX, (OS/SDHF)

Sire: Ch. Tangleloft Odds On Pebwin, CD, WC, (OS)
Dam: Am./Can. Ch. Kinsha's Flight to Rush Hill, (OD)
Whelped: May 17, 1989
Owners: Tonya and Mark Struble, Lake Stevens, Washington

A true Golden gentleman, Kirby is the reward for years of hard work and planning by his breeder-owners, the Strubles. He won his first major at eight months of age and completed his

Rush Hill's Haagen-Dazs is the winner of five Bests in Show and 27 specialties. (Cook Photography)

Championship at one year with three majors. By the time he was 14 months old he had 21 Hall of Fame points and won his first Best in Show at just over two years old.

At eight-and-a-half years of age he has five Best in Show wins and 27 Best of Breed Specialty wins. He is one of the top-winning specialty dogs of all time.

Besides his show career, his natural retrieving abilities and trainability are evidenced by titles in obedience, field and agility. He received his Novice Agility title with nine weeks of training in three straight shows.

To date, Kirby has produced more than 65 champion offspring. Four of these are Best in

Kirby is a working retriever as well as an outstanding show dog. He has titles in field, obedience and agility. (Tonya Struble)

Show winners in this country and several are in the Show Dog Hall of Fame. He passes on his overall body type, movement and temperament to his offspring. They seem to have his confidence and longevity as a show dog.

It is his personality that makes Kirby special. He is truly an ambassador for the breed, as he is gentle, kind and not aggressive. As a show dog, he gets better with age. As a working dog, he tries to do the best job without lots of training or drilling. He is consistent in everything he does, whether it is showing, working or producing.

Ch. Sassafras Batterys Not Incld, (OS/SDHF)

Sire: Am./Can. Ch. Asterling's Jamaica Verdict, (OS/SDHF)
Dam: Ch. Sassafras' Jumpin Jilli Bean
Whelped: March 20, 1988
Owner: Lorraine Rodolph, Marshfield, Massachusetts

Here is another example that the work of the dedicated breeder-owner does pay off. Ready signified

Ch. Sassafras Batterys Not Incld, (OS/SDHF), rewrote Golden history by winning Best of Breed at four national specialties from 1990 to 1995. (Ashbey Photography)

to many breeders that it could be done; a Golden could be a successful special without a major advertising campaign. There were no more than eight ads placed during his career and he was never shown extensively.

Ready completed his Championship at one year of age and went on to be a multi-Best in Show winner and Best of Breed Specialty winner. His greatest achievement is that he was Best of Breed at four GRCA national specialties from 1990 to 1995.

Ready is a "wash and wear" Golden, and a very athletic one. He never needed a treadmill and his exercise consisted of playing with the other dogs or chasing tennis balls.

His contribution as a sire is that when he came on the scene people read the standard again and started breeding for structure. His offspring seem to have inherited his zest for life, which is an important part of his legacy. He is the sire of many Best in Show winners and Show Dog Hall of Fame members.

Throughout his show career he was shown by Linda More and Eileen Hackett, two people who care for the well-being of dogs and are highly respected professionals in the world of dog shows.

(June Smith)

CHAPTER 13

What You Should Know About Breeding

Many years ago, a college student bought a one-year-old AKC-registered Golden female. It was not her first Golden Retriever, but it was the first dog she had owned by herself. Everyone told her what a wonderful dog Rachel was and that she should breed her. Not only should she be bred, but just about everyone said they might be interested in a puppy.

Her owner called her veterinarian's office and they gave her telephone numbers of stud dog owners. Rachel was bred to a local dog before she was two years old. About two months later, nine healthy puppies were born during a stormy night. Rachel did it all on her own without any human assistance. Strangely enough, the people who had said they might want a puppy were no longer interested. So when the pups were about three weeks old advertisements were placed in the newspaper for AKC-registered Golden puppies at $75 each. This was the going price at the time in that part of the country. Most of the callers were interested in a female puppy and these sold quickly. There were some inquiries about whether the sire and dam were OFA-cleared and what their pedigrees were. Rachel's owner had been told that hips did not matter and she had only been given a pedigree of Rachel's dam.

As the puppies got older they were lots of work. There was no suitable place to keep rambunctious puppies that were over seven weeks of age. Desperation began to set in and it was feared that two of the boys would never find homes. When the last two puppies were nine weeks old a woman called who was interested in buying two puppies. Things turned out well after all, and Rachel's owner learned some valuable lessons. The pin money she had been told she would make never materialized. When the bills for food, veterinary costs, advertising and the stud fee were added up, she'd actually lost money.

A few months later she decided to order a complete pedigree for Rachel from the AKC. There were some titles on the pedigree, but she did not know what they meant. For all she knew, CD could have meant Champion Dog! One day at a bookstore she found *The Complete Golden Retriever* by Gertrude Fischer and everything changed. There were dogs in the book that she recognized from Rachel's pedigree, and this led to a desire to learn more about her dog's background. She learned about hip dysplasia, proper breeding practices and about field, tracking and obedience. Life was never the same again.

This is a true story, and Rachel's owner was yours truly.

CANINE OVERPOPULATION

While it may appear at first glance that breeding and raising a litter of Golden puppies is a worthwhile endeavor, it is one that requires more effort than reward. Before undertaking this venture, there are some serious considerations to think over and decisions to be made. The most important of these is that there are too many unwanted dogs in the

world, including Golden Retrievers. You might argue that one litter will not make any difference, but you'd be wrong. If everyone adopted this attitude, the problem would be enormously worse.

Every year thousands of Goldens are abandoned and abused or turned over to animal shelters. The actual numbers of Goldens bred in this country is staggering. During the month of October 1997 just over 1,500 Golden Retriever litters were registered with the AKC, with an average of eight puppies per litter. This ads up to 12,000 Goldens per month. Many of these never show up in AKC figures because they are never registered. The AKC *Stud Book* lists dogs and bitches that produce litters for the first time. Goldens average about 1,000 first-time producers per month. We are talking about some hefty numbers that suggest a population that often exceeds its demand.

The majority of dogs listed in the *Stud Book* have no titles, no recognizable kennel names on the sire or dam and, when you add the fact that fewer than 200 Goldens receive OFA clearances per month, the majority of these dogs lack health clearances of any kind.

Statistics alone are reason enough not to breed without a very good reason. People need sound pets and should be educated in the importance of obtaining a well-bred dog, but as long as poorly bred litters are available for the uneducated buyer, the problem will never improve.

Breeding a litter in the hopes of making money or to finance the purchase of a top show pick or to pay for the career of another dog is never justified. Dogs are not commodities. Buying a bitch and having just one litter for fun is usually no fun at all. The litter produced so the children could experience the wonders of the birth process or for a 4-H project is usually only work for parents and is a litter that was never needed in the first place.

Breeding and raising a litter properly requires time, knowledge and resources. (June Smith)

These are just a few of the many reasons why most people should never breed their dog, but this is just the negative side. You might be further convinced if you look at the positive side and the many requirements that should be met.

GOOD REASONS TO BREED

There is only one real reason to breed a litter, and that is to produce Golden Retrievers of excellent quality. A clear-cut intention to improve the breed should be your sole guide in planning any breeding. This may seem to be too lofty a goal, but it is only through efforts to improve the breed that any semblance of quality can be maintained.

The dogs considered in your breeding program must be outstanding individuals and have highly desirable traits to offer the breed. This type of evaluation is subjective and interpretations vary, but there are basic guidelines you can use.

EVALUATING A DOG FOR BREEDING

The perfect Golden Retriever has yet to be bred. No matter how beautiful a particular dog may be, the ideal dog as described in the breed standard does not exist. Consequently, dogs with minor faults are bred. There are black and white areas where decisions are clear cut, but there are an equal number of gray areas that require judgment calls.

Hips and Elbows

The most obvious place to start is with health and soundness clearances. There are so many Golden Retrievers with hips cleared by the Orthopedic Foundation for Animals (OFA) that there is no reason to consider breeding a dog with hips that do not pass OFA evaluation.

Hip X-rays can be sent to OFA and receive a preliminary evaluation as early as six months of age, but an OFA number is not issued. Breeding should not be based on a preliminary X-ray; a dog's hips often change as they mature. There have been many Goldens bred on the basis of a preliminary X-ray that appeared good, but when X-rayed again at two years of age were dysplastic.

Another method of evaluating hips is the PennHIP system offered through International Canine Genetics. A dog is X-rayed in different positions and actual angles are measured for the degree of laxity of the joint. Numbers are given for both hips based on the Distraction Index (DI). The DI numbers are then interpreted on the basis of where the DI of the hips falls within the range of Golden Retriever hips in the PennHIP database. PennHIP recommends only breeding stock with a DI of less than .30.

PennHIP also rates osteoarthritis as none, mild, moderate and severe (the DJD rating). The diagnosis is based on the combined DI and DJD. Normal hips have a DI of less than .30 and no DJD. A DI of greater than .30 indicates an increased risk of DJD. Hip dysplasia is confirmed with a high DI and the presence of DJD.

This method is based on measurements and numbers and is therefore more objective than with OFA. Dogs can also be accurately evaluated at a much younger age than with an OFA X-ray.

The disadvantages are that to date, a relatively small percentage of the Golden population has

Any Golden considered for breeding should have all of its health and soundness clearances. (Susan Stewart)

been evaluated by PennHIP. Most veterinarians have the equipment and knowledge to take X-rays suitable for OFA, but PennHIP requires specially trained veterinarians that are a part of the ICG program, and there are few of these available. Additionally, the PennHIP method of evaluation is more expensive than OFA.

Elbow dysplasia is another concern when evaluating soundness. This can be done at the same time as an OFA X-ray and is also evaluated by the Orthopedic Foundation for Animals. Elbows receive either a pass or a fail rating, and dog are eligible for official clearance at 24 months of age.

The Eyes

Any Golden considered for breeding should have its eyes examined by a board-certified ophthalmologist. All examinations are sent to the Canine Eye Registration Foundation (CERF). If you send the owner's copy of the ophthalmologist's report along with a minimal fee, you will receive a number that verifies your dog's eye report.

Dogs suffer from many genetic eye problems, but the one of primary concern to Golden breeders is juvenile cataracts. These are triangular occlusions centered on the back side of the lens. They usually appear prior to seven years of age in Goldens. Another common cataract in Goldens is the Y suture cataract.

Central progressive retinal atrophy (CPRA) is uncommon, and its onset and progression are usually gradual. With this disease, the light receptors of the center of the retina deteriorate, leading to blindness. These dogs see life from the sides of their eyes. They adapt so gradually to blindness that owners often never notice their dogs are blind. A Golden diagnosed with cataracts or CPRA will not pass an exam and can not receive a CERF clearance, and obviously should never be bred. Breeding stock should be examined yearly, as cataracts of genetic origin can appear up to seven years of age and beyond.

Irregularities of the eyelashes are observed and noted by ophthalmologists, but a few misplaced eyelashes are not of serious concern. However, severe trichiasis or distichiasis should eliminate a dog from any breeding program. A dog with entropian or ectropian should also never be considered as a breeding prospect.

The Heart

A heart exam by a veterinary cardiologist is another must for any Golden considered for breeding. Subvalvular aortic stenosis (SAS) is a life-threatening condition that is detected by a murmur from the right side of the heart. You'll find more about this disease in Chapter 6, but the main thing to remember here is that dogs that appear free of an SAS murmur should receive a clearance letter from a cardiologist. This can be sent to OFA with a registration fee to receive a clearance number. Dogs diagnosed as having SAS murmurs should not be bred.

Thyroid, Seizures, Skin Problems

A dog that requires thyroid medication should be excluded from breeding. A completely healthy dog that tests at the low end of the normal ranges can be bred with extreme care as part of a well-thought-out program.

OFA now offers a registry for dogs that test free for autoimmune thyroiditis (Hashimoto's disease), which is the most common cause of primary hypothyroidism. This disease usually manifests itself at between two and five years of age. A dog may test low before signs actually develop. A blood sample is sent to OFA, where it is read. The test should be redone at two, three, four, six and eight years of age. The initial fee is $15, and there is no additional fee for recertification.

Goldens with epileptic seizures should not be bred. This is another good reason why dogs should not be bred until they are fully mature. Seizures of genetic origin or predisposition often do not appear until a dog is three years of age.

Dogs with persistent skin allergies also should not be bred. Skin allergies alone are probably responsible for more problems and vet bills than any of the problems I've already listed. While they are environmental, there are also genetic dispositions to skin allergies and they are an indication of a poor immune system.

BEYOND CLEARANCES

The existence of every clearance in the world is still no reason to breed a dog. The clearances only indicate that the dog is free of certain genetic health problems. This has no bearing on whether the dog is a good representative of the breed or on what it will produce. This is the time when anyone considering breeding needs an experienced hand—someone who can make objective comments and help in important breeding decisions. You need a mentor.

Your mentor should be someone with years of experience in dogs. Hopefully, it will be another Golden fancier, but this is not a necessity. There are so many attributes other than health to assess, that a guiding hand and objective eye can make the difference between failure and success for the novice breeder.

Temperament

A Golden should not be bred unless it possesses outstanding temperament. There should be no hint of shyness or spookiness. A Golden that encounters an abnormal situation that might be cause for fright will bounce back to normal immediately.

A Golden should never act aggressively towards people, children or other dogs. It should be friendly, outgoing and predictable in its reactions.

Meeting the Standard

Structurally, the dog should be as balanced and correct as possible. Most structural inadequacies are difficult to correct in a single breeding.

A Golden considered for breeding should possess outstanding temperament and be a good representative of the breed. (Caroline Kaplonski)

Fortunately, most dogs are quite functional with less than perfect angulation. A dog that is seriously defective in the rear, such as severely cow hocked, or very straight in the shoulder or rear should not be bred. A poor topline is an indication of other structural problems.

The head should be as attractive as possible, with pleasant expression, dark eyes, proper ear set and dark pigmentation. Dogs that are overshot or undershot should not be bred; those missing teeth should be bred with great caution.

Is this dog a retriever, as its breed name indicates, or is it merely a gold-colored dog? The natural instincts of a retriever are as much a part of what makes the breed special and unique as its looks, soundness and temperament. A Golden Retriever should love to retrieve, instinctively like birds and be biddable in nature.

One may question the validity of this, when a dog's primary purpose is to be a pet. But it is the looks, combined with certain personality traits, that are the essence of a good retriever and that make the breed what it is. To ignore this is to lose the character of the breed.

Titles earned in the various phases of competition are not reasons to breed. They may be indications that a dog is a good representative of the breed, is trainable, athletic and retrieves birds. But it does not indicate soundness or temperament. You need to evaluate the entire picture. A dog must be completely sound, a good specimen of the breed physically, free of major faults, outstanding in temperament and must possess the traits that make a Golden a retriever. Any minor negative points must be strongly outweighed by positive attributes if you intend to breed the dog.

WHAT MAKES A GOOD BREEDER?

After you have spent considerable time assessing the suitability of your dog as a breeding prospect, it's time to look at yourself. Do you have the traits and resources required to be a good breeder? The term "breeder" goes beyond attaining health clearances, selecting a stud dog and whelping a litter. A breeder must have time, money, knowledge and commitment.

Interviewing, educating and helping prospective buyers and new owners is time-consuming. As puppies get older, their mother will spend less time with them, and this must be made up by the breeder.

Once they are on solid food, their living area will be messy and require frequent cleaning with a sterilizing solution. Their coats will need to be combed regularly. Their nails should be clipped and ears checked and cleaned. The puppies will need more and more interaction with humans after five weeks of age.

The breeder must know how to educate new owners about the needs of a puppy and how to raise a Golden Retriever. They should have a knowledge

Golden litters can be large. This mother appears to be satisfying the needs of her eight puppies, but many cannot. (Janis Teichman)

of problems associated with puppies and be able to recognize when veterinary help is needed.

Breeding a quality litter can be an expensive proposition. There are many more costs in addition to what you'll spend obtaining health clearances and on the stud fee. The obvious requirements of shots, veterinary exams and optional dewclaw removal will run into several hundred dollars, depending on the size of the litter. Unplanned medical problems, such as a cesarean section at the time of birth and puppies that are injured or become ill, can run into thousands of dollars. High-quality puppy food must be purchased when the pups are three to four weeks of age. When this is combined with advertising costs, putting together a puppy information packet and anything else you might send home with a puppy, several hundred more dollars have been spent.

Suitable homes may not be found for all the pups by the time they are seven weeks old. A breeder must be committed to proper placement and be able to hold on to puppies until the right home comes along, rather than placing them any-where. A breeder should also have the facilities, time and money to keep puppies until the right home is found.

Responsible breeders are committed to the dogs they produce for the life of the dog. They should be there to help owners when they have training problems or to offer support if health problems are discovered. They are there to take back the dogs they have bred if the owners can no longer keep them.

A breeder must be mentally and emotionally tough enough to handle the death of a bitch during pregnancy or whelping and the death of puppies. Sometimes puppies must be put down due to deformities, and the breeder must be able to do this. Are you sure you can?

SELECTING A SIRE

If all tests have been passed and all the signals say go, it's time to start thinking about the stud dog.

Advertising a litter is just one of the many expenses of breeding. (American Kennel Club)

This can be an extremely complicated undertaking. If the right dog is not found, or if you discover that you need to overcome too many shortcomings on the part of your bitch, it may be best to stop the search.

You should begin your search by attempting to learn as much about the genetic background of your bitch and her siblings as possible. A complete understanding of your dog's pedigree is in order. You need to know what the various titles mean, who the dogs were and what traits they possessed. This can only be done by researching in books and newsletters and asking questions of those who have been in the fancy longer than you.

You need to do this research as thoroughly as you can, because while dogs exhibit individual physical and mental traits, when they reproduce they are responsible for a gene pool. That is, they are as likely to pass on not only the good and bad traits they themselves possess, but also the good and bad of the dogs closely related to them. This can lead to some pleasant surprises, as well as some unpleasant discoveries. And the unpleasant ones usually crop up more often.

An excellent example of this is often encountered with hip clearances. If a dog is the only individual in its litter that has good hips (assuming all have been X-rayed), it will most likely produce poor hips because that is what is prevalent in its gene pool. A dog with hips rated fair, from a litter where all others have passed with good or excellent ratings, will often be a producer of good hips, especially if the other parent has strong hips.

Learning about the dog's genetic background will help in making educated choices, rather than

Breeders must take responsibility for exposing their puppies to a variety of experiences at a critical early age. (Andrea Johnson)

guessing. A potential sire should have none of the same weaknesses as the bitch, and should be able to compensate with strengths in her weak areas. A bitch with eyes or pigment that need darkening should be bred to a dog with dark eyes and pigment who has littermates and parents with this strength. A bitch that is an excellent marker and stylish retriever but is weak on water retrieves should be bred to a dog that is naturally good in the water.

A dog should never be used just because it is the most popular current stud or the only one available. The dog should be the best one for the bitch in question.

Evaluating a stud dog should begin with health clearances. You should expect as much of the stud dog, in terms of soundness, temperament, retrieving ability and adhering closely to the breed standard, as you do of the bitch. You should be able to see the dog's pedigree and learn as much about his background as you did with your bitch.

Although there are many, many Golden Retrievers in the world, the genetic lines among the best field, show and obedience lines are often very close. Looking at these relationships, you will see cases of outcrossing, linebreeding and inbreeding. Outcrossing is the combination of individuals that share virtually no ancestors in common within five generations. A common dog or two in the fifth generation is still an outcross. Linebreeding is the breeding of loosely related individuals. This can include grandfather to granddaughter, an aunt to a nephew or even cousins. Linebreeding is very common, although family breeding is a better term for what most consider to be linebreeding. Linebreeding should only be attempted by the beginning breeder if every possibility has been researched. Inbreeding is the union of very closely related individuals—mother to son and brother to sister are typical examples. Inbreeding should never be undertaken by anyone other than the breeder willing to cull puppies and keep or place dogs with the utmost care.

A dog should never be selected for the sake of breeding to a particular line or a particular dog that might be in its pedigree. It should stand up on its own merits. If a dog has been bred previously and has offspring, try to see as many of them as possible.

The availability of the dog is an important factor to consider. Will it be necessary to travel long distances or to ship your bitch by air? The use of collected fresh or frozen semen has become increasingly common, and some stud dog owners prefer this method. Some owners no longer breed their dogs naturally due to age, physical injury or fear of infection. However, any time artificial insemination becomes the choice, the chances of actually producing puppies seems to decrease.

The owner of the stud dog is almost as important as the dog. It should be someone you know you can trust in their honesty and their ability to

The ability to produce quality is a trait that cannot be predicted. Research and knowledge can help in making the correct choice. (June Smith)

take care of your bitch if you leave her in their care.

The terms of the stud service should be perfectly clear to both parties. Some stud dog owners want a puppy, others want a fee at the time of the breeding, and still others collect their fee when the litter registration is signed. If a contract is not available, it is a wise idea to draw one up so that there are no misunderstandings.

Raising a litter is hard work for the bitch. Telcey, with her three-day-old puppies, looks tired. (Sue Van Buren)

FINAL PREPARATIONS

All your careful research and evaluation should take place well in advance of your bitch coming in season. You may have been so concerned with research and health clearances that you have forgotten some very simple precautions. All shots should be up to date, so that your bitch provides proper immunity to her puppies during their first few months. She should be free of parasites, both internal and external. The eggs of some worms are often difficult to detect in adult dogs, so if you see no sign in the dog's stool, you still need to have your vet examine it under a microscope. If your dog has been on a flea control regimen such as Advantage or Frontline, you will want to stop these applications prior to breeding. Program, however, can be continued.

At the time your bitch comes into season, she will need a brucellosis test. Brucellosis is an infection that is most commonly transmitted through sexual contact, so this is a courtesy to the stud dog owner and is usually required.

If you are planning to breed by artificial insemination, you will want to have blood samples drawn for progesterone tests as soon as the heat cycle begins. The progesterone level in the blood indicates the best time for a breeding. The test is done every other day until the proper levels are reached. While this is expensive, it can save guesswork and missed breedings. An artificial insemination breeding should not be attempted without these tests. Even if a natural breeding is planned, it can pinpoint the time to breed to the day.

If a bitch is to be shipped, she will also need a health certificate to fly on any airline. You will also need to make airline reservations and plans for the little traveler.

THE MALE AS A STUD DOG

So far my discussion has been aimed at the owner of the bitch. This is because more females are bred than males, and the initial decision to have a litter begins on the distaff side. But a dog should not be offered at stud or bred unless it has met all the criteria I have previously described.

Many people forget that the owner of the male is equally responsible for making breeding decisions. The stud dog owner has every right to refuse service to a bitch. Money for a service easily rendered is a heady inducement, but bitches that are lacking in health clearances and quality should not be bred, and no responsible stud dog owner should profit from an ill-chosen breeding. Even if the bitch is of good quality and has clearances, there is no reason to breed if the stud dog will not improve or compliment her qualities.

If the owner of the bitch is not capable of doing a proper job as a breeder, the breeding should be refused. The stud dog owner is as responsible for the creation of the puppies as the bitch owner, and should be held equally accountable if they are not placed properly.

Breeding dogs is not always simple, and the stud dog owner is responsible for making sure the breeding is accomplished. You can't just put the dogs in the backyard and let nature take its course. There is a lot more to managing a breeding.

First of all, if you accept bitches for breeding, you must have the proper facilities to keep the bitch. Trips to airports and unexpected trips to the veterinarian occur frequently, and some bitches and dogs are difficult to breed. There are bitches that will attack a male dog, and injury is a risk. Infections can develop that result in sterility. Artificial insemination procedures may be in order if a breeding cannot be accomplished naturally. This adds increased time and frustration to a venture that might have seemed simple at first.

It is important to learn as much as possible about the background of a dog before considering breeding. This includes knowledge of littermates, parents and grandparents. (Janis Teichman)

Another problem you must be ready to deal with is that if the puppies are defective in any way or do not meet the expectations of the breeder, it is the stud dog that is always blamed. Adding all this up, it is often hardly worth the stud fee or the effort to stand your dog at stud.

THE ADVANTAGES OF NOT BREEDING

I have looked at the reasons not to breed, the only reason to breed and all of the requirements that should be met. It should be clear that there are many advantages to choosing not to breed your dog. These begin with saved time and money, but there are more.

A Golden that is spayed or neutered faces fewer health risks, such as the likelihood of infections or certain types of cancer. This will save heartache and vet bills in the long run. Neutering also reduces hormone-related aggression and reduces the chance of dog fights. The only thing that a neutered Golden cannot do is reproduce and be shown in conformation. A dog can still be competitive in every other dog-related activity. Most important of all, you have not added to the dog overpopulation problem by producing more puppies.

Breeding a litter is a serious responsibility and a long-term commitment that should never be undertaken lightly. You must have a deep and lasting interest in the Golden Retriever breed and a clear goal in mind of what you want to produce before you even consider becoming a breeder.

BACK TO OUR STORY

So what happened to Rachel? About six months after her owner discovered the world of Goldens, Rachel had been X-rayed and received an OFA "good" rating. Her eyes had been examined by a ophthalmologist and she had a CERF number. They enrolled in obedience and a conformation classes.

Despite an erratic pedigree, Rachel was of finishable quality and there were plans to show her as well as obtain an obedience title. After several years of learning about Goldens and gaining experience in the three available levels of competition, Rachel's owner bred her a final time.

This time things were done right, with proper clearances and plenty of forethought. A sire was selected that lived 200 miles away. He appeared to compliment her and added an extra dose of retrieving ability and trainability that she lacked. The resulting puppies were placed in good homes after long interviews.

While the price of the puppies was considerably higher than the first litter, there were no financial rewards. The gross was greater, but so were the expenses. The only reward was in a job well done and providing properly bred Goldens to loving homes. It was reward enough.

A Golden must be outstanding in temperament and soundness to ever be considered as a breeding prospect. The prospective breeder must have a long-term interest in the puppies they produce and the future of the breed. (Edwina Ryska)

(June Smith)

CHAPTER 14

Caring for the Older Golden Retriever

There is no specific age at which a Golden is considered to be a senior citizen. As a whole, the breed is relatively long-lived when you consider their size. It is not uncommon for Golden Retrievers to reach 16 years of age, although 12 to 14 is a much more realistic expectation. What this means to you is that your Golden will most likely be old for a much longer period of time than it was young.

SIGNS OF AGING

White hairs on the face and muzzle are the most recognizable sign of aging, but this is not true of all Goldens. Some, and especially certain family lines, tend to become gray in the face at a young age. A whitened face can be misleading on a three-year-old dog, but it is not uncommon. This occurs in humans as well, although, like their owners, most Goldens begin to get a sprinkling of white hairs on their head around middle age.

As Goldens mature and the aging process goes into full swing, weight gain may become a problem. This may be due to several factors. The first is a natural slowing down of the body's metabolism with age. The dog becomes less active and needs fewer calories to maintain its normal weight.

Part of the blame may lie with the owner. If the dog's exercise level has been maintained through regular training or planned exercise, and then restricted without adjusting the diet, the dog will gain weight.

Excess weight can cause a dog to age more quickly. Exercise is difficult for an overweight dog, and any physical problems will be worsened by the presence of excess fat on the body.

The body itself is no longer as lithe and agile, even for a dog in good weight. The dog tires more easily when exercised and may be noticeably stiff the next day. This can be due to arthritis in various parts of

Goldens can live to be 16 years old. Consequently, a good percentage of their life is spent as a senior citizen. (June Smith)

The most noticeable sign of aging is a graying face. Ch. Parkewood's Win-Taf Kiss O' Gold, CD, (OD), enjoys retirement. (Kathy Wood)

the body. Tiring can also signal congestive heart problems.

A Golden's hearing will often begin to change as early as six or seven years of age. Their ears will become increasingly sensitive to certain noise ranges. Dogs that were never bothered by thunder or fireworks in the past will exhibit signs of emotional trauma by destroying everything in sight or go into hiding in the safest place they can find. In time, as that part of the hearing scale is lost, they will no longer be sensitive to these noises. Eventually hearing loss progresses to almost total deafness.

The eyesight will also change, although the changes are usually so gradual that they are not recognizable. Clouding of the eyes is a natural aging process not related to cataracts. Vision loss is most apparent in dogs that are regularly worked in some activity that requires

Even though her senses may have diminished with age, Kelly still enjoys the attention of her young friend. (Susan Kluesner)

marking skills or keen visual judgment. A loss of vision is a good signal that retirement is in order.

VETERINARY CARE

Some Goldens never seem to age; they maintain all of their faculties and remain fit and active even though they may be 12 or 13 years old. Even these dogs need special attention, as their bodies may be changing internally without outward signs.

While nothing can be done to prevent vision or hearing loss, we do have some control over other changes associated with aging. As a dog approaches eight or nine years of age, a veterinary exam and blood screen should be done yearly. While a blood screen is not inexpensive, it can spot developing problems before they become critical. The functions of the kidneys and liver can be monitored, and dietary change or a liver supplements may be deemed necessary to correct deficiencies.

Cysts and fatty tumors begin to show up with frequency as a dog ages, and these should be brought to the attention of a veterinarian. Most are benign, but they should always be observed for changes.

If a dog has been diagnosed with hip dysplasia, the arthritic changes associated with this condition may now be noticeable even though the dog has so far led a normal life. Medication to relieve the symptoms of arthritis can be prescribed. When a Golden with hip dysplasia becomes older it is especially important that it not become overweight. Not all arthritis is associated with hip dysplasia, either. It can appear anywhere in the body, including the spine.

Yearly vaccines must be maintained and stool samples tested for the presence of internal parasites. Illnesses common to dogs, such as parvovirus and kennel cough, are of the most consequence to very young dog and older dogs.

GROOMING THE OLDER GOLDEN

The older Golden will probably need more grooming than it did during its earlier years. As a Golden ages, its coat becomes increasingly dense. Such coats retain more moisture and dirt and mat more easily than their youthful editions. The dog will need more frequent regular brushing, with special attention paid to hot spots if that has been a problem in life. Baths should only be given indoors or when it is warm outdoors, and the dog should be thoroughly dried before going out in the cold. Taking care to dry a dog thoroughly in cold weather is always important, but is even more so for the older dog. An older dog should never be left wet in an unheated area, as this can lead to pneumonia.

The nails seem to grow faster and require more frequent clipping in an older dog. This is because the oldster is not as active, and the natural wear that kept the nails shorter when the dog was young is no longer occurring. Most older Goldens prefer to be indoors, and nails are not worn down by carpet and linoleum.

As a dog ages, the teeth show the wear of years of chewing. The teeth may appear as no more than stubs. The oral fixations of youth often diminish as a dog ages, and while this is good in certain respects, it is detrimental to the teeth. The chewing action helps to keep teeth clean and prevents the build-up of plaque and the gum disease that results from it. If regular care of the teeth has not been part of your dog's normal regimen, it should now be added.

COMMUNICATION

Some vision and hearing loss can mean ordinary commands or signals are not seen or heard. A dog that cannot hear the command to come or sit will not respond. If you have trained your dog to respond to hand signals, this can make up for much of the deficit. The signals taught for Utility-level obedience work well, or you can devise your own.

Special care should be taken to make sure the older Golden is thoroughly dried after bathing or swimming. (Janis Teichman)

There is no reason why an older deaf dog cannot be taught hand signals by moving the dog into the correct position with physical praise or a food reward as you give the signal. A hand motion towards the chest can mean come, the hand moved upwards from the waist might signify sit, and a hand motion made towards the ground might mean down.

The next difficulty is in getting a dog's attention when it is not looking in the right direction. Stamping your foot can send vibrations that the dog feels and may work to get its attention. Sometimes there is no other choice than to physically get the dog. This should lead you to the conclusion that extra care must be taken for the safety of the deaf or sight-impaired dog. They are in a world of their own and cannot hear whistles or commands to come if they wander away and become lost.

Older dogs often become more communicative in attempts to get their demands met. Some dogs that were silent in their youth learn to express themselves by barking when they are hungry or want to come inside. As their hearing may be reduced, they are not even aware of how loud they are. The best thing is to satisfy their demands and keep them in the house.

THE DIET

It is a misconception that a dog must be put on a food designed to meet the needs of old age. If a dog has been fed a quality food with proper ratios of ingredients for a dog of moderate activity level, the older dog can remain on that diet. If the dog is beginning to gain weight, you can feed the dog less or increase its exercise. If the dog is incapable of exercise, a diet that restricts fats and proteins is certainly in order, but if all functions are normal and the dog is in good health and weight, it can be kept on regular food.

If blood tests indicate a special diet is needed, an appropriate change should be made. Special diets for older dogs allow you to feed the same amounts without putting more weight on the dog. Dog foods high in protein and designed for puppies or very active working dogs should never be fed to an older dog, as these can lead to kidney failure.

EXERCISE

The amount of exercise a dog needs or wants varies greatly from dog to dog, and must be approached on an individual basis. Extremely

Older Goldens enjoy nap time, and a comfortable spot is important to old bones. (Janis Teichman)

active, self-motivated dogs will usually remain that way as they age. An extremely lazy Golden that gains weight easily should receive regular exercise to keep the body moving and prevent weight gain. If physical restrictions prevent the running and jumping that they are used to, a less strenuous form of exercise should be continued.

The best exercise for any older dog is walking. It provides movement without undue stress to the body. Swimming is another good form of recreation that provides exercise without making too many physical demands.

It is always amazing what an old dog is capable of physically when it really wants something. Sara was a 13-year-old field trial retiree who spent her days dreaming of ducks, but only getting an occasional bumper. One day she was with her owner and two dogs as they were walking beside a pond after a day of field training. Sara spotted a pair of ducks and dove into the water with her two friends close behind. The two other dogs were called back and placed under control, but Sara, due either to deafness or "selective hearing," ignored commands to come.

It seemed funny at first as the ducks kept swimming around the pond, just out of reach of the gray-faced Golden. But after the third trip around the big pond it became obvious that the dog was not going to give up her pursuit. Finally, Sara's owner swam out to catch her. She expected an out of breath, exhausted dog, but Sara was calm and her heart beat steadily and slowly. If anything, she was mad because her chase had been interrupted. The important thing was that this marathon swim was possible not just because of Sara's desire, but because she was not overweight and had been kept fit and active through a combination of planned exercise and her own high activity level.

These are the companion years. At no other time in a Golden's life is it so easy to live with or able to provide such friendship. (Laurie Berman)

THE PUPPY AND THE OLDER DOG

At some point, most people who own a Golden contemplate adding a second one to the family. This becomes particularly important as you see your favorite dog enter the last years of its life. The pain of losing a dog and the void their passing creates in our lives is unbearable. Adding a puppy is one way to lessen the pain and ease the transition. As it grows, the new puppy becomes a continuation of your relationship with your old dog, through its knowledge of and association with that dog.

Some Goldens love puppies, but this is not necessarily true of all of them. Puppies can be obnoxious and bothersome to an older dog.

The older dog may feel its position in the household threatened by the presence of the newcomer and react protectively. It will want to protect

Sunburst's Lil-Pot-O'Gold, CDX, TD, JH, WCX, pictured at 12, enjoyed life to the fullest for over 13 years. (Bliss Glazebrook)

There is so much an older dog can teach a young puppy. (Janis Teichman)

its sleeping area, its toys and its people from what it perceives to be nothing more than a little monster. Usually though, after a period of adjustment the older dog will learn to love its new little friend.

If a new puppy is to be brought to the house, make the older dog a part of the process. If the puppy is picked up from a local breeder, take the older dog along so that it can see where the pup is coming from. Introduce them to each other at a neutral location. Hold the puppy in your lap and let the older dog sniff it, making the adjustment gradual.

In your home, give the puppy its own area and restrict it from the areas the older dog inhabits. This would include a special room and sleeping and eating areas. The puppy should not be allowed around the older dog when it is eating or chewing on a bone or anything else considered to be personal property. This is when injury to a puppy is most likely. As lovable as we all believe our dogs are, all it takes is one warning snap that accidentally lands on a little skull or an eye to cause permanent damage. Until the puppy is older, it should never be left alone with the older dog, no matter how much they seem to like each other.

If you find your older dog really does not like this intruder, you will need to be patient with the acceptance process. Most older dogs learn to live with the new puppy when it begins to take on adult proportions at four to six months of age. Sometimes all it takes is getting the dogs together in a location away from home for them to get along.

The addition of a puppy is a wonderful way to add years to an old dog's life. They now have a playmate and begin to act like puppies themselves. The older dog acts as a role model for the puppy by showing it how to behave and react to new and different situations. If the old dog comes when it is called and gets a treat or attention, the puppy learns by imitation. Beware, though, because bad habits can be learned in the same way, such as excessive barking and fear of certain noises.

WHAT CAN AN OLDER DOG DO?

There is no reason why an older dog that still enjoys working cannot participate in some form of competition. There are even classes designed specifically for older dogs. The national specialty

Am./Can. Ch. Golden Pine's Courvoisier, CDX, WCX, (OS), competed in obedience and the field, and had Group placements well after his tenth birthday. (Janis Teichman)

Wraith's Duncan, MH***, (OS), relaxes over a glass of wine at the table with his owner. (Rosita Wraith)

and some obedience trials offer veteran obedience classes. Most specialty shows offer conformation classes for veterans, as well.

Field trials are too demanding for dogs much over the fittest 10-year-old, but hunting tests are well within the abilities of an athletic older dog.

Older dogs make excellent therapy dogs, as they are calmer and gentler than a younger Golden.

The later years of a Golden's life are often the best years of a long relationship. This is the period when the dog truly becomes a companion and its greatest joy is the time spent under the desk or lounging on the couch while its owner works. An older dog may make fewer demands, but it has the same needs and requires as much care and time as the younger Golden, if not more.

(Elaine Maloit)

CHAPTER 15

The Golden Retriever Club of America

T he primary purpose of a national breed club is to unite owners and breeders in the common cause of protecting and improving a breed. The Golden Retriever Club of America, Inc., (GRCA) is one of the largest and most influential breed clubs in the country. Its strength and influence is furthered by the many regional member clubs that sponsor GRCA-related activities locally.

The stated purpose of the GRCA and every member is to breed Golden Retrievers that possess the soundness, temperament, natural ability and personality described by the standard and to advance and promote these qualities in a sportsmanlike manner according to the rules of the American Kennel Club.

Promoting the breed was the main objective when the GRCA was formed in 1939. The breed had been registered for just over 15 years and had only been recognized as a separate AKC breed for the last seven years—since 1932. The first Golden Field Champion was not made until 1939, and at this time only 22 Goldens had earned their breed Championship. The first Field Champion was bred in this country, but two-thirds of the breed Champions were of Canadian or British origin. There were very few Goldens and even fewer fanciers, but they were dedicated in their efforts for the breed and their resolve to form a national club.

Before the GRCA was formed, Golden fanciers communicated through the breed column in the *AKC Gazette*. With the club came a breed publication to air concerns and generate ideas. National specialty shows came next. The first was held in 1940 in Wisconsin. There were 45 entries in the breed classes and 44 total entries in the field trial. An obedience trial was not added until 1950.

The concerns of GRCA members at that time differed greatly from ours today. Too much popularity and indiscriminate breeding were not on the agenda. The early Golden fanciers were looking for recognition and a market for the puppies they bred. Health and soundness concerns were directed at diseases that no longer exist, such as hard pad, or are now under control through vaccination, such as rabies and distemper. Golden fanciers did not yet know about hip dysplasia or cataracts. Golden Retrievers were bred solely because they were outwardly good representatives of the breed.

Members of the GRCA strive to breed Golden Retrievers that possess soundness, good temperament and natural ability. (Janis Teichman)

ONE BREED

The one concern that continues to haunt all serious Golden owners and breeders is echoed in the thoughts of the first GRCA president, John K. Wallace of the St. Louis, Missouri, area. He bred and owned both field and bench champions. His major fear, even in the early years of the breed, was that it remain one breed. In other words, the Golden should be a dog that is not only a good representative of the breed standard, but that can also perform the duties of a hunting dog. It should never be two separate breeds, with show specimens lacking retrieving instinct and field dogs bearing little or no resemblance to the dog described in the standard.

In the pursuit of keeping the dual nature of the Golden Retriever, the GRCA has from its inception strongly promoted field events. It has always included a field trial at its national specialty, hosts an all-breed field trial, and promotes basic field ability with its Working Certificate program.

The GRCA has grown over the last six decades, and now hardly resembles the little club of the 1940s. Through the efforts of the GRCA, soundness problems were brought to the attention of Golden owners and breeders and steps were made to bring these under control through screening procedures. This has brought about routine X-rays for hip dysplasia and the formation of OFA. Concerns about cancer, epilepsy and SAS have all been brought to the forefront through the efforts of the GRCA. In 1997 the GRCA adopted a Code of Ethics for all Golden owners and breeders (you'll find it in Appendix B).

ETHICS AND EDUCATION

The education of Golden Retriever owners and potential owners has become an increasing concern of the GRCA. Education projects have been undertaken in an attempt to control overpopulation and to make sure people understand the commitment and responsibility Golden ownership requires.

The first attempt at reaching all owners of registered Goldens was the Public Awareness Letter (PAL) sent out in 1989. Every owner of a newly AKC-registered Golden was sent a one-page letter outlining the purpose and needs of the breed, breeding guidelines and information on the GRCA. This was accomplished with the cooperation of the AKC. This expensive but worthy attempt was eventually abandoned, but with a revised edition of the PAL and renewed help from the AKC, the program has resumed in 1998.

Education is a primary concern of the GRCA and its member clubs. This is an information booth at the Erie County Fair, staffed by members of the Western New York Golden Retriever Club. (Laurie Warner)

The GRCA continues to publish inexpensive pamphlets and booklets on the breed. These are available for as little as 10 cents apiece through the national club and can be handed out or sent to anyone interested in owning or breeding Goldens. A new manual on acquiring a puppy should be available soon, as well as one on forming a rescue group.

The real task of education is the responsibility of every GRCA member and begins with the screening of puppy buyers and calls from people interested in breeding their pet bitches.

THE NATIONAL SPECIALTY

The GRCA National Specialty is an annual event of tremendous proportions. At the 1997 specialty in St. Louis, Missouri, 1,647 dogs were entered in the show, with 305 of these in obedience, 216 in field trials and 151 in the Working Certificate program. There was also a tracking test and an agility trial.

Another event that everyone looks forward to at the specialty is the Parade of Titleholders. This is open to Champions of record in field, show and obedience, Utility Dogs and Master Hunters. One of the greatest honors is to own the oldest dog in the titleholders parade.

The national specialty lasts about a week. Besides the competitive events, there is an

The Veterans classes are large and very competitive at the national specialty. Ch. Parkewood's Win-Taf Kiss O'Gold, CD, (OD), is examined by the judge. (Kathy Wood)

educational seminar, the yearly national meeting, an awards banquet and an auction to raise money for Golden Retriever Rescue. It is the biggest Golden Retriever party in the world, and an event that every Golden Retriever owner should experience at least once. The national specialty is held in a different city every year, and is hosted by one of the member clubs in the three zones that divide the GRCA. It moves from the Eastern zone to the Central to the Western and then back to the Eastern zone. This gives Golden owners in all parts of the country an equal chance to participate.

In addition to the national specialty, each zone holds an annual regional specialty hosted by a member club. The regional specialty is usually a single day or weekend event and is more limited in

The GRCA National Specialty is one of the largest single breed events every year. (Cook Photography)

Success at the 1995 national specialty field trial. Tom Lehr and Pine Run's Some Buddy, MH**, WCX, with Reserve JAM in the Qualifying; Jim Drager and Pine Run's Top Gun, CD, MH***, WCX, with a JAM in the Open and Qualifying and Bart Schlachter and Buffy's King of Hearts, MH***, second place in the Qualifying at 11 years of age. (Jim Drager)

its scope, offering conformation, obedience and a Working Certificate test.

Individual clubs also host independent specialties. The activities offered at these events are restricted to breed and obedience competition. They may be held in conjunction with an all-breed show or as an individual event.

SPECIAL AWARDS

The GRCA offers more than 34 perpetual special trophies for outstanding achievement in various fields. These are awarded at the banquet held in conjunction with the national specialty. To be eligible, the owner of the dog must be a GRCA member. There are more than one dozen trophies awarded for points accumulated in field, show and obedience competition over the course of a year. The two oldest trophies have been awarded since 1938: The Gilnockie Challenge Trophy is awarded to the owner with the Golden earning the highest number of field trial points; the Rockhaven Speedwell Pluto Trophy is awarded to the owner of the dog with the best record in AKC conformation shows, based on the number of dogs defeated. The oldest obedience award is the Toby-Trigger Trophy, which honors the owner of the Golden that has earned the most points from placements in AKC obedience trials.

The remaining two dozen or so trophies are awarded for special achievements at the national specialty. The oldest field award, going back to 1940, is the FC Rip Trophy, which goes to the owner of the winner of the Open All-Age stake. There are at least six other field trophies.

The Wochica's Okeechobee Jake Trophy was awarded to the owner of the Best of Breed winner, but was retired and replaced in 1993 with the GRCA Best of Breed Trophy. The Mud Creek Flare UD Trophy is awarded to the owner of the highest-scoring Golden in the obedience classes. This trophy dates back to 1960.

THE HALL OF FAME

The GRCA recognizes the outstanding accomplishments of Goldens as producers and in three areas of competition. An Outstanding Sire or Dam must have produced a required number of offspring with advanced titles. Before 1986, only a Championship, UD, or Field Championship (FC or AFC) were recognized. But the requirements have

Splashdown Texas Two Stepper*** won the FC Rip Trophy in 1996 and 1997. In 1996 she took a double header, also winning the Amateur All-Age stake. (Jim Pickering)

of Fame is the smallest in size, with fewer than 100 Goldens over nearly a 60-year history. A dog enters the Field Dog Hall of Fame by earning points in All-Age competition. Placements at the Group level are required for the Show Dog Hall of Fame, and entering the Obedience Hall of Fame is determined by High in Trial awards won. The specific requirements for each are described in Appendix D.

VERSATILITY AWARDS

The GRCA recognizes accomplishments in a variety of fields with Versatility Certificates (VC). This program was revised in 1997 to include the agility program and new tracking titles. Qualification is now based on a point system. A dog needs at least one point from conformation, field or obedience competition and a total of six points overall for a Versatility Certificate. This could be fulfilled with a

since been significantly altered to reflect the additional activities and titles now offered and the accomplishments of the dog with titles in more than one area of competition. Titles earned from AKC hunt tests, field trial achievements (other than an FC or AFC), tracking and agility all have a bearing on Outstanding Producer status.

The requirements for the respective Field, Obedience and Show Dog Hall of Fame have remained relatively unchanged. The Field Dog Hall

Emberain Hunthill Rain Beau, SH, WCX, returns with a duck. (Barbara Taylor)

Championship (four points), CD (one point) and JH (one point). A dog that has received championship points in combination with titles is also eligible for a VC.

The Versatility Excellent Certificate (VCX) is awarded to dogs that have earned a total of 10 points from titles. This might include major show points (three points), a UDT (five points) and a WCX (two points). Receiving the VCX is not automatic upon earning titles. The dog's owner must apply to the certificate chairperson with the appropriate proof of titles for recognition.

THE WORKING CERTIFICATE

The Working Certificate (WC) test was first offered in the 1960s by the GRCA as a way of testing a dog's natural retrieving abilities, as opposed to those acquired through training. The idea was that Golden owners who did not have the time or money to run field trials could prove their dog still possessed the qualities of a working retriever.

The overall rules are based on Derby and Qualifying field trial rules, with some modifications. In the late 1970s the Working Certificate Excellent Test (WCX) was added to recognize the ability that comes with more advanced training, as well as natural ability.

The Working Certificate consists of one test on land and one in water. The land test is a simple double mark with the bird landing about 40 to 50 yards from the line (where the dog and handler are located) in moderate cover. The falls should be at least 90 degrees apart. The birds may already be

Can. Ch. Waynewood's Captain Nemo, CD, WC, and handler on the line at a Working Certificate test. Note that the handler lightly holds the collar, which is permitted at this level. (Laurie Warner)

dead or a live flyer may be shot as the last bird down.

One can expect pigeons or pheasants on a land test. The gunners will be clearly visible, wearing light-colored clothing. The dog can be held by light restraint on the line, but cannot leave or be sent to retrieve until the judge has given a signal to release it. The handler cannot touch the dog between being sent for birds, nor can the dog be touched to take a bird out of its mouth. A dog does not have to retrieve to hand (that is, hold the bird in its mouth until it is willingly released to the handler). It must, however, bring the bird back to an area close to the handler that has been previously designated by the judges.

The water test consists of two single marks in swimming water, with the ducks thrown 25 to 30 yards from the line in light cover. Again, the dog must not leave until sent and must return to a designated area with the bird.

These are simple situations that test the basic instincts of the Golden. It must be able to use its eyes and nose to find birds. The double is included to indicate memory and intelligence, a very important ingredient in any retriever. The dog must be able to retrieve a bird while swimming in water and willingly re-enter the water for a second bird.

A dog may fail the test because it is unable to find a bird or return to the designated area. A dog that switches (finds a bird, drops it to pick up another bird, or goes to one area to hunt but leaves it to go to the area of another bird) has failed. A dog that refuses to enter the water, does not go when sent or eats the bird will also fail.

A dog that successfully completes the test receives a certificate issued by the GRCA and can place the initials WC after its name.

The Working Certificate Excellent test is much more difficult in its scope and requires a considerable amount of training. The land test is a triple using upland game birds. These three falls can be thrown in a right to left or left to right order, and are between 60 and 100 yards from the line. The falls should be no less than 60 degrees apart. The water test consists of two freshly killed ducks thrown at distances of 45 to 60 yards from the line, with an honor. The memory mark must be in cover with at least one mark in water deep enough

to swim in. A live shot duck can be used as the last bird down.

A dog must be steady, though a controlled break (a dog goes before being sent, but comes back to heel position with a quick command) is allowed. It must come to the line and leave the line off leash and under control. The dog must deliver to hand and cannot be touched at any time. All of the causes of failure mentioned in the WC test apply.

It should be mentioned that these are marking tests and a dog that is handled or helped to the bird in any way cannot pass. The WCX was devised to indicate advanced marking and training skills. Preparation for a WCX test takes a considerable amount of time in teaching obedience in field situations and marking and memory skills beyond

The Working Certificate Excellent test requires more training and control. Dogs must be steady, retrieve to hand and cannot be touched or restrained at any time. (Andrea Johnson)

natural ability. A dog that passes this test can add a WCX after its name.

The rules applying to WC and WCX tests can be obtained through the GRCA. A WC/WCX test is held at the national specialty, regional specialties and once a year by many local Golden Retriever clubs.

PUBLICATIONS

The number one reason to belong to the GRCA is the *Golden Retriever News*, the bimonthly club publication. It is eagerly awaited and read from cover to cover several times until the next issue arrives. For many GRCA newcomers it is a reason for living.

An average issue is 200 pages long. It contains pertinent GRCA news and articles about health, breeding and educational topics. There are sections on conformation, field, obedience, agility and tracking that provide information for the novice and experienced trainer. There are many advertisements, which give ample opportunity to learn about Goldens and breeding programs throughout the country. It is the voice of the GRCA, and the quality of this publication never lets up from issue to issue.

Another publication of the breed club is the *GRCA Yearbook*. This is published every other year and records the accomplishments of every Golden in AKC competition over the two-year period. Dogs earning advanced titles and Hall of Fame status are pictured, along with a three-generation pedigree. It is an excellent reference for anyone interested in learning more about Goldens or searching for information about the background of particular dogs on a pedigree. Yearbooks can be obtained from the beginning of the breed club. They contain the history of the Golden Retriever in this country.

GOLDEN RETRIEVER RESCUE

No other area of GRCA involvement has grown so quickly and received so much attention as breed rescue. Initially this was an undertaking of a few dedicated individuals and local clubs. The GRCA

National club events, whether in conformation or performance, always attract a large group of keen competitors from all over the country. (American Kennel Club)

now raises thousands of dollars for rescue through donations and its annual raffle. The GRCA formed the Committee to Assist Rescue, but the bulk of rescue work still lies with the local Golden clubs.

The purpose of breed rescue is to find homes for Goldens that are no longer wanted by their owners or are found abandoned or turned in to animal shelters. Almost all rescue work is done by volunteers. Their energies are spent answering telephone calls, transporting animals, grooming, administering care, providing temporary homes, raising funds and a endless list of other tasks. These services usually go unappreciated and unrewarded.

Many heartbreaking stories of Goldens given up to rescue groups have very happy endings. (Elaine Maloit)

behavior in 1995, with almost half of these euthanized because they were not placeable.

There are many heartbreaking stories associated with rescue—dogs that are found injured and abandoned, starved and abused. The majority of rescue cases, however, involve fairly well cared for dogs whose owners simply can no longer keep them for a variety of reasons. The number one reason for placing a Golden is lack of time, followed by moving, with unmanageable or aggressive behavior close behind.

A rescue operation requires money. It takes money to pay phone bills, travel expenses, food and

A survey published in 1996 in the *GR News* gives a clear picture of the scope and activity level of Golden rescue organizations across the country. At that time there were 45 active rescue groups with 826 volunteers. A total of 3,146 dogs were rescued during the year. This was up by more than 1,000 dogs from both 1993 and 1994. The most active organizations were NorCal GR Rescue with 373 dogs, and Yankee GR Rescue with 275! There were 270 dogs turned in due to aggressive

veterinary bills. During 1995 Yankee Golden Retriever Rescue spent $80,000 in its efforts. Several other clubs were close behind. The average annual expenses for a rescue group of moderate activity come to about $25,000. The money required is raised through auctions, raffles, the sale of specialty items and donations. All of these activities require organization and volunteers.

One of the most ambitious undertakings of any rescue group bore fruit in 1997. Yankee

On reflection, no one could have foreseen 60 years ago that the Golden Retriever would become so popular or that rescue organizations would ever become necessary. (Janis Teichman)

Golden Retriever Rescue, which has been the prototype for Golden rescue organizations, purchased its own facilities. This is a large old home on 21 wooded acres outside of Boston that has been licensed as a kennel. This will serve as a central location to keep rescue dogs until they can be placed and may provide boarding services in the future to owners of Yankee rescue dogs. The home itself will provide office space and meeting rooms.

Yankee makes much of its income by selling Golden goodies. These are items that feature Golden Retrievers or are of direct interest to owners of the breed. The new location will provide a storage place for these items and a center to fill orders. More dog runs will be added to those already in existence. This has all been made possible through hours of dedication, hard work, and a clear goal and vision for the future.

Most rescue organizations are not as fortunate. Lack of funds and help cause burn-out in many volunteers. It can be extremely depressing listening to people who no longer want their Golden. It may be easy to find a home for a puppy, but not for a big male with no training and bad habits, or an old dog that requires special care. Some rescue dogs require extensive veterinary care to restore them to health and must be cared for until they are ready for adoption.

Almost anyone involved with rescue has taken a dog into their own home until a permanent home can be found. This should not be done unless the dog can be isolated from the resident dog population for a period of quarantine. Taking a dog on a temporary basis is always disruptive to the normal routine. People do it because they love the breed.

The founders of the GRCA never envisioned a club of such size, nor a breed that would become so popular, nor could they foresee the need for rescue in 1939. The GRCA has constantly adapted and adjusted to the growing needs and changes that have occurred over the years. The GRCA offers something for almost anyone interested in or concerned about Goldens. Information about the club can be obtained by calling the telephone number listed in Appendix A.

(American Kennel Club)

Epilogue

Golden Retrievers have been in the public eye for more than 20 years. We have seen them in the White House, they have been important characters in movies and television shows and they are seen in advertisements every day.

There are some very good reasons for this exposure, and it speaks well of the breed. Goldens are beautiful dogs with great eye appeal. They are easy to train and can learn to perform many tasks well. The down-side of this exposure is that the people who see these dogs never see the hours of training that went into creating such perfection.

The images of dog ownership portrayed in recent movies that feature Golden Retrievers are not positive ones. Shadow (the Golden) and his friends Chance and Sassy in the *Homeward Bound* series of movies do not have a fenced yard. Their owners leave them with little thought for their welfare. If they had been cared for properly, the premise for these movies would have never existed. The Golden in the recent movie *Air Bud* lives in squalid conditions and escapes to a situation that is no doubt better. However, his new home does not have a fenced area and we see him fed food that is not suitable for a dog. The consequence of these images is that there are many people who believe they want a Golden, based solely on what they've seen presented in the media.

The path to popularity was first paved when Liberty became a resident of the White House during President Gerald Ford's administration. Liberty was from excellent breeding, but regardless of her actual quality, she was a pet. She was bred to the great field trial Golden FC-AFC Misty's Sungold Lad, CDX, and this White House litter of puppies received nationwide attention.

Liberty may have had her hips X-rayed, but she did not have an OFA number. OFA readings were common even 25 years ago in Goldens. The impact on the breed was twofold: It brought Goldens into the public eye, and it made breeding Goldens and producing cute puppies like the ones in the White House fashionable. One can only speculate about how things might have been different if Liberty had been spayed, or if news of her litters had been accompanied by information about obtaining proper health clearances.

Goldens are frequently recommended by veterinarians and other dog professionals because they make good family dogs. The potential buyer, in their search for a Golden, is armed with no other knowledge than this statement. They are almost always looking for an inexpensive puppy and it does not matter if there are papers or even if the dog is purebred. The assumption is that if the dog is even part Golden Retriever, it will make the perfect pet.

Because they just want a pet, this buyer usually passes up the well-bred litters in favor of the bargain puppy. Sometimes this works out, but the Golden from an indeterminate background may not be such a bargain after all. This is obvious when one listens to the comments of owners of pet Goldens. Remarks such as, "my Golden weighs 125 pounds," "our Golden is very sweet, but she has terrible skin problems, which is why her first owners probably got rid of her" and "our male Golden is nine months old and we are having a hard time controlling him" are commonplace. Too many people just don't realize that finding the right Golden requires knowledge and research.

The price of popularity is that people who have no business owning a dog, let alone a Golden Retriever, are now Golden owners. They have never been properly educated about responsible dog ownership, nor about the proper rearing and care of a Golden.

Thousands of Goldens are bred every year by this same type of person, which only perpetuates the problem and leads to a decline in the quality of the average Golden that the uneducated pet buyer purchases. In the eyes of the public, the Golden becomes a breed that is hyperactive, prone to skin problems and lacking in overall soundness. Any

All well-bred Goldens should be outgoing, friendly and find joy in life. (Elaine Maloit)

responsible breeder will readily admit that they have produced an occasional skin problem or an unruly puppy, but they are also available to assist and educate the owner of that dog.

There is a wide range of types within the breed. Goldens differ greatly in their size, color, coat and energy levels, yet all can be deemed good representatives of the breed. The unifying trait of the Golden Retriever is its temperament. The Golden is outgoing, friendly and predictable in its reactions. Anyone looking for a Golden should always keep this all-important fact in mind.

There are some excellent reasons to obtain a Golden. They are wonderful companions and their addition to a home is like adding a family member. They will want to be a part of their new owner's life. They are outstanding in many areas of activity and are happiest when given a purpose in life. Obtaining a Golden for the children, or because they are pretty and mellow dogs, are not good reasons to get one.

We live in a world where dog ownership is increasingly becoming a privilege and not the right we once believed it to be. There are several powerful organizations in this country whose true agenda is the eventual elimination of all pets. They may profess to serve the welfare and protection of animals, but their ultimate aim is to eradicate animals from our lives. Such groups have influence that extends to officials that set local ordinances and run animal facilities. Their causes, which are

aimed at restricting ownership and breeding of dogs, are well received by people who see nothing but irresponsible dog owners. This includes those that neglect their animals and allow them to roam and produce unwanted puppies. When one only sees this side of the story, their view is naturally biased.

In many counties and cities, dog ownership has become severely restricted. Producing litters is subject to fines or increased fees. In many states extremely restrictive measures have been placed before legislatures that could radically change the sport of purebred dogs. This is why responsible dog ownership is so crucial. Responsible ownership

All Golden owners are guardians of the breed and its unique temperament and abilities. (Janis Teichman)

includes proper licensing, providing proper care and a fenced yard, and spaying and neutering all pets and pet-quality dogs. It does not stop there. All dogs should receive proper obedience training and should never be considered a nuisance to the community. We should always be an example of the best and serve as ambassadors, not only for the Golden Retriever, but for all purebred dogs.

Facing this challenge is a growing concern for responsible Golden Retriever owners and breeders.

The future of the breed and how it adapts to the ongoing stress of over-popularity is a part of our immediate future. There is no breed of dog that is as physically attractive or talented in so many areas as a Golden. They are an active, intelligent dog, and while they are suitable for many people, they were never meant to suit the needs of everyone. A sound and healthy Golden with a typical temperament is easy to care for and train, and a delight to live with. May this always be true.

Resources

American Kennel Club
5580 Centerview Drive, Suite 200
Raleigh, NC 27606
(919) 233-9767
www.akc.org

AKC Breeder Referral Service
(900) 407-7877

HomeAgain, AKC Companion Animal Recovery
5580 Centerview Drive, Suite 250
Raleigh, NC 27606-3394
(800) 252-7894
www.akc.org

American Dog Owners Association
1654 Columbia Turnpike
Castleton, NY 12033
(518) 477-8469
www.global2000.net/adoa/

American Temperament Test Society
P.O. Box 397
Fenton, MO 63026
(314) 225-5346

AVID Microchip I.D.
(800) 336-AVID
www.avidplc.com

Canine Companions for Independence
P.O. Box 446
Santa Rosa, CA 95402-0446
(707) 577-1790
www.caninecompanions.org

Canine Eye Registration Foundation (CERF)
South Campus Courts, Building C
Purdue University
West Lafayette, IN 47907
(317) 494-8179
www.vet.purdue.edu/~yshen/cerf.html

Delta Society Pet Partners
289 Perimeter Road East
Renton, WA 98055
(800) 869-6898
www2.deltasociety.org/deltasociety/

Dogs for the Deaf, Inc.
10175 Wheeler Road
Cental Point, OR 97502
(541) 826-9220
www.dogsforthedeaf.org

Golden Retriever Club of America, Inc.
(281) 861-0820, club information
(Contact the AKC for the current club secretary
address)
www.grca.org

Guide Dogs for the Blind
P.O. Box 151200
San Rafael, CA 94015
(415) 499-4000
www.guidedogs.com

Love On A Leash
P.O. Box 6308
Oceanside, CA 92058
(619) 724-8878

North American Dog Agility Council
HCR 2 Box 277
St. Maries, ID 83861
(208) 689-3803
www.teleport.com/~jhaglund/nadachom.htm

North American Flyball Association, Inc.
1400 W. Devon Avenue
Box 512
Chicago, IL 60660
(309) 688-9840
muskie.fishnet.com/~flyball/flyball.htm

**North American Hunting Retriever
Association**
P.O. Box 6
Garrisonville, VA 22463
(703) 752-4000
starsouth.com/nahra/

National Association for Search and Rescue
4500 Southgate Place, Suite 100
Chantilly, VA 20151-1714
(703) 222-6277
www.nasar.org

Orthopedic Foundation for Animals (OFA)
2300 Nifong Boulevard
Columbia, MO 65201
(573) 442-0418
www.offa.org

PennHip/International Canine Genetics
271 Great Valley Parkway
Malvern, PA 19355
(610) 640-1244 or (800) 248-8099

Therapy Dogs, Inc.
P.O. Box 2786
Cheyenne, WY 82003
(307) 638-3223
home.ptd.net/~compudog/tdi.html

Therapy Dogs International
6 Hilltop Road
Mendham, NJ 07945
(201) 543-0888

United Kennel Club
100 East Kilgore
Kalamazoo, MI 49001-5598
(616) 343-9020
www.ukcdogs.com

U.S. Dog Agility Association
P.O. Box 850955
Richardson, TX 75085-0955
(214) 231-9700
www.usdaa.com

Golden Retriever Club of America Code of Ethics

The Golden Retriever Club of America endorses the following Code of Ethics for its members. It is the purpose of the GRCA to encourage its members to perfect through selection, breeding and training the type of dog most suitable in all respects for work as a companionable gun dog, and to do all in its power to protect and advance the interests of Golden Retrievers in every endeavor.

RESPONSIBILITIES AS A DOG OWNER

Members must ensure that their dogs are kept safe and under control at all times. Members should properly train their dogs so that they are an asset to their community and not a nuisance. Dogs must be maintained with their safety and good health in mind at all times, including adequate and appropriate attention and socialization, grooming, feeding, veterinary attention, housing, routine care, exercise and training.

RESPONSIBILITIES AS A MEMBER OF GRCA

Members' responsibilities include educating the public about the breed, keeping in mind that they and their dogs represent the breed, the GRCA and the sport of purebred dogs in general.

Members are urged to accept the written breed standard as approved by the American Kennel Club (or the other applicable governing body of the country in which they reside or exhibit) as the standard description of physical and temperamental qualities by which the Golden Retriever is to be judged.

Members are required to maintain good sportsmanship at all events and competitions, abiding by the applicable rules and regulations set forth by the governing bodies of such events and competitions. Members' conduct should always be in accord with the purposes and intent of the GRCA Constitution and By-Laws.

(Janis Teichman)

RESPONSIBILITIES AS A BREEDER

GRCA members who breed Golden Retrievers are encouraged to maintain the purpose of the breed and are expected to demonstrate honesty and fairness in dealing with other owners and breeders, purchasers of dogs and the general public. Owners of breeding animals shall provide appropriate documentation to all concerned regarding the health of dogs involved in a breeding or sale, including reports of examinations such as those applying to hips and eyes. If any such examinations have not been performed on a dog, this should be stated.

Breeders should understand and acknowledge that they may need to take back, or assist in finding a new home for any dog they produce at any time in its life, if requested to do so.

Members who breed should sell puppies, permit stud service, and/or lease any stud dogs or brood bitches only to individuals who give satisfactory evidence that they will give proper care and attention to the animals concerned, and who may be expected generally to act within the intent of the statements of the Code of Ethics. Members are encouraged to use clear, concise written contracts to document the sale of animals, use of stud dogs, and lease arrangements, including the use, when appropriate, of non-breeding agreements and/or Limited Registration. Members should not sell dogs at auction, or to brokers or commercial dealers.

ADVISORY GUIDELINES

Breeding stock should be selected with the objectives of GRCA in mind. That is:

Recognizing that the Golden Retriever breed was developed as a useful gun dog, to encourage the perfection by careful and selective breeding of Golden Retrievers that possess the appearance, structure, soundness, temperament, natural ability and personality that are characterized in the standard of the breed, and to do all possible to advance and promote the perfection of these qualities. (Paraphrased from Article 1, Section 2, of the GRCA By-Laws, as amended in 1995.)

GRCA members are expected to follow AKC requirements for record keeping, identification of animals, and registration procedures.

Animals selected for breeding should:

(i) Be of temperament typical of the Golden Retriever breed; stable, friendly, trainable, and willing to work. Temperament is of utmost importance to the breed and must never be neglected.

(ii) Be in good health, including freedom from communicable disease.

(iii) Possess the following examination reports in order to verify status concerning possible hip dysplasia, hereditary eye or cardiovascular disease.

a. Hips—appropriate report from Orthopedic Foundation fro Animals; PennHIP; Ontario Veterinary College; BVA/KC Hip Score (Great Britain) or at least a written report from a board certified veterinary radiologist (Diplomate of the American College of Veterinary Radiologists).

b. Eyes—appropriate report from a Diplomate of the American College of Veterinary Ophthalmology (ACVO) or from a BVA/KC-approved ophthalmologist (Great Britain).

c. Hearts—appropriate report from a Diplomate of the American College of Veterinary Medicine, Cardiology Specialty.

Consideration should be given also to other disorders that may have a genetic component, including, but not limited to, epilepsy, hypothyroidism, skin disorders (allergies), and orthopedic disorders such as elbow dysplasia and osteochondritis.

(iv) Assuming all health and examination reports are favorable, the age of the breeding pair is also of consideration. Generally a Golden Retriever is not physically and mentally mature until the age of two years; an individual dog's suitability as a breeding animal is difficult to assess until that time.

Adopted: April 20, 1997, by the GRCA Board of Directors.

(Andrea Johnson)

Titles a Golden Can Earn

AMERICAN KENNEL CLUB TITLES

Conformation and Dual Titles

Championship titles always precede a dog's name.

Ch.	Conformation Champion
DC or Dual Ch.	Conformation and Field Champion
TC	Triple Champion (CH, FC and OTCh)
CT	Champion Tracker

Obedience Titles

Titles for obedience and other performance events come after a dog's name.

CD	Companion Dog
CDX	Companion Dog Excellent
UD	Utility Dog
UDX	Utility Dog Excellent
OTCh	Obedience Trial Champion

Field Titles

FC	Field Champion
AFC	Amateur Field Champion
FC/AFC	FC and AFC
JH	Junior Hunter
SH	Senior Hunter
MH	Master Hunter

Tracking Titles

TD	Tracking Dog
TDX	Tracking Dog Excellent
VST	Variable Surface Tracking Dog

Combination Titles

UDT	Utility Dog Tracker
UDTX	Utility Dog Tracker Excellent

Agility Titles

NA	Novice Agility
OA	Open Agility
AX	Agility Excellent
MX	Master Agility

Canine Good Citizen

Although CGC is an AKC program, the title is not officially recognized. While you may put it after the dog's name, it will not appear on an official AKC pedigree.

CGC	Canine Good Citizen

Golden Retriever Club of America Titles

GRCA titles are placed after a dog's name, usually after the AKC titles. These titles are not recognized by the AKC.

SDHF	Show Dog Hall of Fame
OBHF	Obedience Hall of Fame
FDHF	Field Dog Hall of Fame
OD	Outstanding Dam
OS	Outstanding Sire
VC	Versatility Certificate
VCX	Versatility Certificate Excellent
*	Placement in Sanctioned Field Trial
**	Placement in Field Trial, Derby or Qualifying
***	First or second place in qualifying or a JAM in a Championship stake
WC	Working Certificate
WCX	Working Certificate Excellent

UNITED KENNEL CLUB TITLES

All UKC titles precede a dog's name.

U-Ch	Champion
U-CD	Companion Dog
U-CDX	Companion Dog Excellent
U-UD	Utility Dog
HR	Hunting Retriever
HR Ch.	Hunting Retriever Champion
GRHR Ch.	Grand Hunting Retriever Champion
U-AGI	Agility One (Novice)
U-AGII	Agility Two (Advanced)
U-AGIII	Agility Three
U-ACh.	Agility Champion

CANADIAN KENNEL CLUB TITLES

Most CKC titles are the same as those used by AKC, with the following exceptions:

OTCh.	The same as an AKC Utility Dog
FTCh.	Field Trial Champion
AFTCh.	Amateur Field Trial Champion
WC	Working Certificate
WCI	Working Certificate Intermediate
WCX	Working Certificate Excellent
ADC	Agility Dog of Canada
AADC	Advanced Agility Dog of Canada
MADC	Master Agility Dog of Canada

NORTH AMERICAN HUNTING RETRIEVER ASSOCIATION TITLES

NAHRA titles are usually placed before the dog's name.

SR	Started Retriever
WR	Working Retriever
MHR	Master Hunting Retriever
GMHR	Grand Master Hunting Retriever

NORTH AMERICAN DOG AGILITY COUNCIL TITLES

NAC	Novice Agility Certificate
OAC	Open Agility Certificate
EAC	Elite Agility Certificate
NATCh.	NADAC Agility Champion

Titles are also available for different classes, such as Gamblers and Jumpers. These would be NGC, OGC, EGC and so on.

UNITED STATES DOG AGILITY ASSOCIATION TITLES

AD	Agility Dog
AAD	Advanced Agility Dog
MAD	Master Agility Dog
JM	Jumpers Master Dog
GM	Gamblers Master Dog
SM	Snooker Master Dog
RM	Relay Master Dog
VAD	Veteran Agility Dog
ADCh.	Agility Dog Champion

NORTH AMERICAN FLYBALL ASSOCIATION TITLES

FD	Flyball Dog
FDX	Flyball Dog Excellent
FDCh.	Flyball Dog Champion
FM	Flyball Master
FMX	Flyball Master Excellent
FMCh.	Flyball Master Champion
FGDCh.	Flyball Grand Champion

OTHER TITLES

TD	Therapy Dog
TDI	Therapy Dog International
TT	Temperament Test of the ATTS
SKC Ch.	States Kennel Club Champion
UCI Int. Ch.	International Champion, earned in the U.S.
Int. Ch.	International Champion

COMMON ABBREVIATIONS USED AT DOG EVENTS

BIS	Best in Show
BOB	Best of Breed
BOS	Best of Opposite Sex
BISS	Best in Specialty Sweepstakes
BOSS	Best of Opposite Sex Specialty Sweepstakes
WD	Winners Dog
WB	Winners Bitch
RWD	Reserve Winners Dog
RWB	Reserve Winners Bitch
BW	Best of Winners

JAM	Judge's Award of Merit (used in dog shows and field events)	OAA	Open All-Age Stake (field events)
Reserve JAM	JAM that is fifth place	AAA	Amateur All-Age stake (field events)
HIT	High in Trial	LAA	Limited All-Age stake (only Qualified All-Age dogs may compete)
HC	High Combined (from Open and Utility obedience classes)		

(Janis Teichman)

The GRCA Hall of Fame

The Golden Retriever Club of America Hall of Fame recognizes the achievements of Goldens that are outstanding producers or are outstanding in their respective areas of competition: show, field or obedience.

There are so many Goldens in the Hall of Fame that listing them would be a book in itself. For example, in 1996, 24 dogs were named Outstanding Sires and 44 bitches became Outstanding Dams. In an average year, about 12 dogs become eligible for the Show Dog Hall of Fame and 24 for the Obedience Hall of Fame. There are currently 90 dogs in the Field Dog Hall of Fame since its inception 50 years ago, for an average of two field dogs qualifying a year.

To enter the GRCA Hall of Fame in any discipline, a dog must meet certain requirements based on points.

OUTSTANDING SIRE AND DAM

The requirements for Outstanding Sire and Dam are effective as of January 1, 1998.

To be awarded an Outstanding Sire (OS), a sire must have a minimum of five qualifying progeny who have earned a total of 24 title points, with the following stipulations:

A. No more than two of these progeny may qualify by earning a combination of a three-point title (SH, CDX, OA, TDX, **) and a two-point title (JH, WCX, CD, NA).

B. The remaining qualifying progeny must earn a four-point title (CH, UD, MH, AX) or higher.

To be awarded an Outstanding Dam (OD), a dam must have a minimum of three qualifying progeny who have earned a total of at least 15 title points, with the following stipulations:

A. Only one of these progeny may qualify by earning a combination of a three-point title (SH, CDX, OA, TDX, **) and a two-point title (JH, WCX, CD, NA).

B. The remaining qualifying progeny must earn a four-point title (CH, UD, MH, AX) or higher.

Outstanding Sires and Dams will also include any dog or bitch that has produced two Field Champions (FC or AFC) or one Field Champion (FC or AFC) in combination with one conformation Champion or one UD or one MH or one AX.

Title points will be calculated according to the following schedule:

nine points—FC and AFC

six points—SDHF, OTCH, CT, FC or AFC

five points—UDX, VST, ***, MX

four points—CH, UD, MH, AX

three points—CDX, TDX, SH, **, OA

two points—CD, JH or WCX, NA

one point—TD, WC

Non-competitive titles, such as hunt tests and WC/WCX, earn points only once. Consequently, a dog does not earn four points for a JH and a WCX, but only two points. A dog with an SH and WCX earns three points, not five.

SHOW DOG HALL OF FAME

Any Golden Retriever that earns 25 or more points, based on the following system, will be entered into the GRCA Show Dog Hall of Fame. The point system is as follows:

Best in Show—10 points, plus five points for Group First

Sporting Group First—five points

Sporting Group Second—three points

Sporting Group Third—one point

Sporting Group Fourth—half a point

National Specialty Best of Breed—five points

Regional Specialty Best of Breed—three points

Independent Specialty Best of Breed—one point

Points earned at Regional and Independent Specialties are eligible only if these are not held in conjunction with an all-breed show.

FIELD DOG HALL OF FAME

Any Golden Retriever that accumulates a total of 25 points or more based on its performance in Licensed Field Trials will automatically be entered in the GRCA Field Dog Hall of Fame. Any Golden Retriever that wins the National Field Trial or National Amateur Field Trial will also be included.

OBEDIENCE HALL OF FAME

Any Golden Retriever with a Utility Dog title that has accumulated five Highs in Trial, of which no more than two have come from the Novice class, will be entered into the GRCA Obedience Dog Hall of Fame.

(American Kennel Club)

National Specialty Winners

All titles listed are those the dog had at the time of the win. The abbreviations I've used are BOB (Best of Breed), BOS (Best of Opposite Sex), High in Trial (High in Trial, obedience), HIAT (High in Agility Trial), AAA (Amateur All-Age stake, field trial) and OAA (Open All-Age stake, field trial).

58TH ANNUAL NATIONAL SPECIALTY

September 29–October 5, 1997
Gray Summit, Missouri

BOB	Ch. Salyran Take It To The Limit Breeder: Sally and Lindsey Cavness Owner: Sally Cavness, Jane Fish and Betsy Strohl
BOS	Ch. Summits Carrera Dom Perignon Breeder: Beth Johnson and Jeanette Ratajczak Owner: Jan Draper and Beth Johnson

HIT	Tanbark Blaze 'N Boots Breeder: Yvone Tobey-Piefer Owner: Sandra Ladwig
HIAT	Colabaugh's Tattle Tail Breeder: Renee and Walter Massey Owner: Beth Iannucci

AAA   Topbrass Ascending Elijah ***
       Breeder: J. and J. Mertens, and
       J. and J. Powers
       Owner: Connie and Brian Cleveland, and
       Judy Rasmuson

OAA   Splashdown Texas Two Stepper ***
       Breeder: Richard and Cynthia Williams
       Owner: Jim and Kathy Pickering

57TH ANNUAL NATIONAL SPECIALTY

September 8–15, 1996
Newark, Delaware

BOB   Ch. Summits Carrera Dom Perignon
       Breeder: Beth Johnson and Jeanette
       Ratajczak
       Owner: Jan Draper and Beth Johnson

BOS   Ch. Lovejoy's Catch Me If You Can Can
       Breeder: Paula Parker and Carol Lovejoy
       Owner: Carol Lovejoy

HIT   OTCh Shoreland Rainier Rambo
       Breeder: Suzanne Mayborne
       Owner: Andrea Vaughan

AAA   Splashdown Texas Two Stepper ***
       Breeder: Richard and Cynthia Williams
       Owner: Jim and Kathy Pickering

OAA   Splashdown Texas Two Stepper ***
       Breeder: Richard and Cynthia Williams
       Owner: Jim and Kathy Pickering

56TH ANNUAL NATIONAL SPECIALTY

September 12–20, 1995
Rohnert Park, California

BOB   Ch. Sassafras Batterys Not Incl'd
       Breeder–Owner: Lorraine Rodolph

BOS   Ch. Rush Hill's Colorful Rumor
       Breeder: Mark and Tonya Struble,
       Randy and Trudy Schepper
       Owner: Susan Babich, Tonya Struble and
       Carol Boitano

HIT   OTCh DD's Calaveras Sparklin' Gold
       UDX
       Breeder: Dee Dee and Billy Anderson
       Owner: Janet Naylor

AAA   Wraith's Hunter Moon Kirby ***
       Breeder: Herbert and Joan Marsh
       Owner: Charles and Rosita Wraith

OAA   Emberain Better Believe It ***
       Breeder: Ed and Edwina Ryska
       Owner: Susanna Kecskemethy

55TH ANNUAL NATIONAL SPECIALTY

October 14–23, 1994
Oklahoma City, Oklahoma

BOB   Ch. Sassafras Batterys Not Incl'd
Breeder–Owner: Lorraine Rodolph

BOS   Ch. Brandymist Q B Gal
Breeder: James and Pamela Cobble
Owner: William and Marie Wingard, and
James and Pamela Cobble

HIT   Ch. Breakwater Ice Capade
Breeder–Owner: Pauline Czarnecki

AAA   AFC Glenhaven Devil's Advocate, UDT,
MH, WCX
Breeder–Owner: Glenda Brown

OAA   FC-AFC Valhaven's Smoke'N Vindaloo
Breeder: Mary Maurer
Owner: Ronald Wallace and
Judy Rasmuson

54TH ANNUAL NATIONAL SPECIALTY

September 7–9, 1993
Kerhonkson, New York

BOB   Am./Can.Ch. Edgehill Nautilus
Calypso Joe
Breeder: Christina Weeks and
Julie MacKinnon
Owner: Jeff Chaffin

BOS   Ch. Golden Pine Tres Cherrybrook
Breeder: Brenda and Eric Wood
Owner: Nancy Kelly and Eileen Oshiro

HIT   OTCH Stardust Rainier Rocky
Breeder: Michael J. MacDonald
Owner: Andrea Vaughan

AAA   Mioak's Keifer Ginger Snap, MH ***
Breeder: Mickey Strandberg
Owner: Susan Kiefer

OAA   Caernac's No Problem ***
Breeder: Sandra Whicke
Owner: Mimi and Frank Kearney

53RD ANNUAL NATIONAL SPECIALTY

October 17–24, 1992
Plano, Texas

BOB   Am./Can. Ch. Asterling's Wild Blue Yonder
        Breeder–Owner: Mary Burke

BOS   Golden Pine Tres Cherrybrook
        Breeder: Brenda and Eric Wood
        Owner: Nancy Kelly and Eileen Oshiro

HIT   OTCH Lochnor B Fifty-Two Bomber
        Breeder: Lockie Treanor
        Owner: Nancy Patton

AAA   Mistfield Red Zinger ***
        Breeder: Mickey Kendrigan
        Owner: Jerrie Heiner

OAA   FC-AFC Topbrass Tyonek
        Breeder: Jackie Mertens
        Owner: Ronald Wallace and
        Judy Rasmuson

52ND ANNUAL NATIONAL SPECIALTY

September 22–24, 1991
Kansas City, Missouri

BOB   Ch. Sassafras Batterys Not Incl'd
        Breeder–Owner: Lorraine Rodolph

BOS   Ch. Peppercreek Sweetest Taboo
        Breeder–Owner: Paul and
        Kathleen Scoggin

HIT   Char-tine Encore E'Clat Edward
        Breeder: Charlene Kay Wilson
        Owner: Deborah and Gary Platt

AAA   FC-AFC Stony-Brooks' Jersey Devil
        Breeder: Carol Lilenfeld
        Owner: Robert and Marjorie Meegan,
        and Jackie Mertens

OAA   Deerhill Iditarod ***
        Breeder: Brian and Barb Pashina
        Owner: Judy Rasmuson and
        Ronald Wallace

51ST ANNUAL NATIONAL SPECIALTY

September 9–10, 1990
Frederick, Maryland

BOB   Ch. Sassafras Batterys Not Incl'd
        Breeder–Owner: Lorraine Rodolph

BOS   Ch. Mardovar's Savannah Star
        Breeder: Doranne Borsay and Chris Jany
        Owner: Janeen Rice and William J. Feeney

HIT   Heron Acres Sand Dollar UDT, JH
        Breeder: Elizabeth Drobac
        Owner: Constance and Elizabeth Drobac

AAA   Skylab's Jedi ***
        Breeder: Tom Cartmill
        Owner: Jerrel and Kathryn Meitzler

OAA   FC-AFC Valhaven Smoke'N Vindaloo
        Breeder: Mary Maurer
        Owner: Ronald Wallace and
        Judy Rasmuson

50TH ANNUAL NATIONAL SPECIALTY

September 10–16, 1989
Boulder, Colorado

BOB Am./Can. Ch. Alderbrookes Rush Hill
Rebel, TD
Breeder: Carole Kvamme
Owner: Tonya and Mark Struble

BOS Ch. Beaumaris Timberee Tessa Ann,
UDT, WC
Breeder: Ann Bissette
Owner: Sandy and Bob Fisher

HIT OTCh Kuventre Dogwood Flower
Breeder: Sharon Long
Owner: Bonnie Baker

AAA FC-AFC Valhaven Smoke'N Vindaloo
Breeder: Mary Maurer
Owner: Ronald Wallace and
Judy Rasmuson

OAA FC-AFC Windbreakers Mighty Mo
Breeder: Pat Denardo
Owner: Stan and Jerrie Heiner

49TH ANNUAL NATIONAL SPECIALTY

September 22–24, 1988
Waukesha, Wisconsin

BOB Ch. Libra Malagold Coriander
Breeder: Cheryl Blair
Owner: Dr. Patricia and Thaddeus Haines,
and Connie Gerstner

BOS Am./Can. Ch. Carlin Happy Holidays
Breeder: Carlin J. Chapley and
Claire Winski
Owner: Kim D. Mortensen and
Carlin J. Chapley-Rasmussen

HIT OTCh Meadowpond Keepin In Stride
Breeder: Cherie Berger
Owner: Theresa Arnold

AAA FC-AFC Windbreakers Smoke'N Zigzag
Breeder: Pat Denardo
Owner: Joseph and Jackie Mertens

OAA AFC Sangamo Red
Breeder: Darrell Frisbie
Owner: Harold Bruninga

Bibliography

BOOKS ABOUT GOLDEN RETRIEVERS

Bauer, Nona, *The World of the Golden Retriever*, TFH Publications, Neptune City, NJ, 1993.

Fischer, Gertrude, *The New Complete Golden Retriever, Second Ed.*, Howell Book House, New York, 1984.

Foss, Valerie, *Golden Retrievers Today*, Howell Book House, New York, 1994.

Nicholas, Anna Katherine, *The Book of the Golden Retriever*, TFH Publications, Neptune City, NJ, 1983.

Pepper, Jeffrey, *The Golden Retriever*, TFH Publications, Ocean City, NJ, 1984.

Schlehr, Marcia, *The New Golden Retriever*, Howell Book House, New York, 1996.

BOOKS ON FIELD TRAINING

Quinn, Tom, *The Working Retrievers*, E.P. Dutton, Inc., New York, 1983.

Rutherford, Clarice, *Retriever Puppy Training*, Alpine Publications, Loveland, CO, 1988.

Rutherford, Clarice, Sandy Whicker and Barbara Branstad, *Retriever Working Certificate Training*, Alpine Publications, Loveland, CO, 1986.

Spencer, James, *Retriever Training Tests, Second Ed.*, Alpine Publications, Loveland CO, 1997.

Walters, Ann and D.L., *Training Retrievers to Handle*, Interstate Book Manufacturers, Olathe, KS, 1979.

Walters, Ann and D.L., *Charles Morgan on Retrievers*, October House, Inc., Stonington, CT, 1974.

BOOKS ON BEHAVIOR AND HEALTH

Carlson, D.G., DVM, and James M. Giffin, MD, *Dog Owner's Home Veterinary Handbook*, Howell Book House, New York, 1994.

Dunbar, Ian, PhD, MRCUS, *Dog Behavior: An Owner's Guide to a Happy, Healthy Pet*, Howell Book House, New York, 1998.

Fogle, Bruce, DUM, MRCUS, *The Dog's Mind*, Howell Book House, New York, 1990.

Rutherford, Clarice and David Neil, *How to Raise a Puppy You Can Live With*, Alpine Publications, Loveland, CO, 1981.

The Monks of New Skete, *How to Be Your Dog's Best Friend*, Little Brown, Boston, 1978.

BOOKS ON OBEDIENCE, TRACKING AND AGILITY

Bauman, Diane, *Beyond Basic Dog Training*, Howell Book House, New York, 1986.

Johnson, Glen, *Tracking Dog, Theory and Methods*, Arner Publications, Westmoreland, NY, 1975.

Simmons-Moake, Jane, *Agility Training: The Fun Sport For All Dogs*, Howell Book House, New York, 1991.

Volhard, Joachim and Gail Fisher, *Training Your Dog: A Step by Step Manual*, Howell Book House, New York, 1984.

BOOKS ON GENERAL REFERENCE, STRUCTURE AND CONFORMATION

Alston, George G. with Connie Vanacore, *The Winning Edge: Show Ring Secrets*, Howell Book House, New York, 1992.

American Kennel Club, *The Complete Dog Book, 19th Edition, Revised*, Howell Book House, New York, 1998.

Elliott, Rachel Page, *The New Dogsteps*, Howell Book House, New York, 1983.

Hutt, Frederick B., DVM, *Genetics for Dog Breeders*, W.H. Freeman and Co., San Francisco, 1979.

Schlehr, Marcia R., *A Study of the Golden Retriever*, Travis House, Flat Rock, MI, 1994.

PERIODICALS

The Golden Retriever News
This national publication of the GRCA is available with club membership. Call (281) 861-0820 for information.

The Golden Retriever Review
S34 W. 32725 Sierra Pass
Dousman, WI 53118
(414) 392-3076

AKC Gazette and *Events Calendar*
5580 Centerview Drive
Raleigh, NC 27609-0643
(919) 233-9767

Retriever Field Trial News
   4379 S. Howell Avenue, Suite 17
   Milwaukee, WI 53207-5053
   (414) 481-2760

Gun Dog Magazine
   P.O. Box 343
   Mt. Morris, IL 61504-0343
   (800) 800-7724

Front and Finish, The Dog Trainers News
   P.O. Box 333
   Galesburg, IL 61402
   (309) 344-1333

VIDEOS

American Kennel Club, *The Golden Retriever*, 21 minutes.

Elliott, Rachel Page, *The Golden Retriever*, 31 minutes. Available from the GRCA, c/o Debbie Ascher, P.O. Box 60, Berthoud, CO 80513-0069.

Yankee Golden Retriever Rescue, *Golden Moments*, 20 minutes. Available from YGRR, Inc., P.O. Box 808, Hudson, MA 01749.

Index